Dilemmas in Truth and Science

Inquiries in the Midst of the Science Wars

by

Timothy McGettigan

Table of Contents

To the Reader

Though it may not appear so at first glance, the chapters that follow are all of a piece. Each is part of a larger endeavor to evaluate the role and veracity of truth in the realm of science. During the 1990s, when I composed the majority of these projects, postmodernists appeared to gaining the upper hand in the Science Wars. To put it bluntly, postmodernists had declared that science was evil and truth was dead. Although certain elements of the postmodern critique clearly had merit, the broader implications for truth and science were more problematic.

In the chapters that follow, I develop a critical analysis of the philosophy and practice of science. While I acknowledge the ticklish problems that coercive power often exercises over knowledge, ultimately, I arrive at a very different conclusion than postmodernists about the value of truth and the future of science.

CHAPTER ONE

Uncorrected Insight[1]

From Confusion to Clarity on the Green Tortoise

Abstract

Postmodernists have criticized scientific truth for serving as a means to impose Western ideology around the globe (Lemert, 1991, 1999; Seidman, 1991). Nevertheless, Fluehr-Lobban (1995) points out that under-defining truth compromises human rights by surrendering limitations upon coercion. In this paper, I advance a "redefined" (McGettigan, 1998a, 1999a) version of truth that, I argue, is well suited to update the criteria of "good science."

Introduction

In this paper, I document experiences from a Green Tortoise adventure in order to advance a "redefined" version of scientific truth (McGettigan, 1997, 1998a, 1998b,1999a, 2000). The discussion begins with a description of my initial orientation to the Green Tortoise—which was rooted in an uncritical acceptance of standard research practices. However, an unanticipated emergency altered my perspective profoundly. During a crossing of the Rio Grande, a male Tortoise passenger allegedly pitched a Mexican rowboat operator and a female passenger into the river. Although the boat operator made it to shore, Amanda[2], the female passenger, disappeared downstream. I dove into the river to render assistance, but in doing so lost my glasses. Thus, my optical vision became blurred for the balance of the journey. However, my jump into the river also clarified my perspective.

In choosing to intervene as a "real" participant, I transgressed a number of barriers (Wichroski, 1996) that I had erected for the purposes of doing "good science" (Dahl, 1957; Denzin, 1994; McGettigan, 1998a). Ironically, by unintentionally contravening the boundaries that I had assumed would *preserve* the validity of my research, my uncorrected vision precipitated a redefinition of reality (McGettigan, 1998a, 1999a) that generated insights of utmost lucidity.

---

[1]   This is an updated version of an article that was originally published in Sociological Research Online: http://www.socresonline.org.uk/6/2/mcgettigan.html
[2]   All personal names have been substituted with pseudonyms.

Field Research on the Green Tortoise

The site of my research project was a fourteen day, San Francisco to New York, adventure trip on the Green Tortoise in October of 1993. The Green Tortoise is a bus travel company, based in San Francisco, that emerged from the youth countercultures of the 1960s. During the sixties a number of small companies offered cross-country bus trips as alternatives to mainstream carriers (e.g., Greyhound, Trailways). The Tortoise outlived its upstart competitors by converting its routine cross-country trips into adventures.

Photo 1. The Green Tortoise

The philosophy of the Green Tortoise (i.e., Arrive inspired, not dog tired) is to elevate the status and comfort of being on the road. This is achieved in part by remodeling each of its buses with cushioned, wood-crafted benches, tables, and platforms. Also, the Tortoise's open seating arrangement encourages the uninitiated to get acquainted rapidly. Last but not least, the Tortoise is also equipped with its own provisions and kitchen. Thus, most basic creature comforts are well tended on a Green Tortoise adventure.[1]

---

[1] Also see Neumann (1993) for an account of a trip that he took in 1987.

Photo 2: An Interior Shot of the Tortoise

Many of the 1960s countercultures failed due to organizational dilemmas (Kanter, 1972). Nevertheless, since then a variety of unconventional businesses—such as food co-ops, neo-communes, alternative newspapers, coffee houses, etc.—have attempted to strike a balance between organizational viability and a rejection of mainstream culture (Rothschild-Whitt, 1979). These organizations embrace conventional business practices to raise operating funds, but they also eschew such activities to avoid compromising their subversive philosophies. The Green Tortoise is an excellent example of a countercultural organization because it is a successful business that is predicated upon a celebration of the rowdy, youthful times from whence it came (Wolfe, 1968). Thus, the Tortoise is clearly connected to mainstream culture, but its unconventional image also typifies a compromised rejection of society.

Initially, I planned to ride the Tortoise as a "participant-as-observer" (Gold, 1958), i.e., a semi-detached participant, for three reasons: 1. To acquire an empathetic (Douglas, 1976) feel for the Tortoise experience; 2. To maintain observational distance, and; 3. To avoid reactive effects (Emerson, 1983, p. 100). In other words, in service to scientific validity (Belgrave and Smith, 1995; Kvale, 1995; Lather, 1995), I wished to maintain a problematic balance (Thorne, 1979, p. 73). I planned to participate in, but avoid contaminating (Richardson, 1994) on-board events.

This strategy emerged out of various unquestioned commitments that I subscribed to as "good" scientist (Dahl, 1957; Denzin, 1994; McGettigan, 1998a). In my role as a "good" researcher, I envisioned my job would be *to observe* others, whereas the primary activity of those I observed would be *to experience* the Green Tortoise. I imagined that this distinction would be subtle enough to permit inconspicuous interaction, but also sharp enough to maintain requisite observational detachment. It was as though I planned to attend an avant-garde play wherein I, the lone audience member, had to ensure the actors remained heedless of their performances. Having determined the parameters of my involvement, I turned my attention to getting in (Pollner and Emerson, 1983).

Tension and Intolerance on a Neo-Hippie Bus

One of the unique features of the Green Tortoise is that "getting in," or what Wax (1971) refers to as "the first and most uncomfortable stage of fieldwork," is equally difficult for all. Field researchers often study well established groups, and, prior to initiation, they appear to be hopelessly inept outsiders (Evans-Pritchard, 1940; Malinowski, 1967; Mead, 1966). However, on the Tortoise there was no pre-established community. Instead, all of the passengers were cast into the role of bungling outsiders.

In fact, developing a cohesive in-group is one of the principle elements of Tortoise journeys. Adventure travel on the Tortoise is predicated upon cramming overbooked passengers onto old, refurbished buses and taking them on long trips without precise itineraries. Because the buses are usually very crowded (e.g., there were forty-two passengers on this journey) passengers are forced to violate many of the niceties of conventional crowd behavior. Sean, a passenger on his sixth adventure trip, noted that a common saying on the Green Tortoise is "Move your meat, lose your seat." Nevertheless, I was alarmed throughout the first few days because of how often I bumped into others and invaded their space—no matter how ill-defined.

Further elevating onboard tension, the drivers, named Curt and Arthur (who appeared to be charter members of the Flower Power movement) kept asserting that we would all benefit by shedding our inhibitions. Many of the women felt particularly threatened by such comments—rolling their eyes, crossing their arms, and shaking their heads in good-natured disgust—especially when the drivers advocated nudity and sex.

 The drivers often spoke reverently of their exploits with uninhibited, sex-crazed passengers, and, indeed, they did more than preach. Whenever the opportunity arose—and it did regularly—the drivers demonstrated their disdain for social norms by shedding their clothing. Curt, the lead driver, professed that his advocacy of sex and nudity derived from a deep-seated resentment of mainstream social repression. According to Curt, discomfort with sex and nudity was simply the result of a warped, socially-imposed sense of privacy and decency.

In keeping with this attitude, the design of the Tortoise invokes routine assaults on passengers' personal space and privacy. When a woman objected to having a man nearby while she changed clothing, Curt vetoed her by shouting "Hey, we're all people!" In fact, there was little sense in seeking privacy on the bus. Passengers had a choice between changing clothes in the semi-privacy of outhouses or roadside bushes, or abandoning discretion and changing in public. Regardless, the Tortoise also found ways to undermine "decency" off the bus as well.

Photo 3: A Desert Stopover

Although the Tortoise visits many conventional places (e.g., truck stops, grocery stores, freeways, national parks), it also travels to many unconventional destinations. On day two, we traveled to a remote, cactus bestrewn corner of the Mojave Desert called Deep Creek Hot Springs. Despite initial enthusiasm, many passengers were alarmed to learn that the springs were "clothing optional." At that stage, few of the passengers—least of all the females—felt comfortable about swimming nude. While Curt gamely took advantage of the no-clothing option, several witnesses disapproved indignantly of his behavior.

The tension and intolerance resulting from such flagrant violations of social conventions made all the passengers wary observers. This heightened guardedness created an effect that was opposite of the intended Tortoise experience (i.e., a friendly, tolerant traveling community). The passengers became exceedingly conscious of the barriers that normally maintain social distances and privacy—and clung to them doggedly.

I got the feeling, as I observed the passengers' vigilance, that we were all going to be outsiders forever. Anyone who behaved too casually was viewed with much the same suspicion as the drivers. When Sean hazarded a swim without his bathing suit, I heard Karl, another male passenger, snarl derisively "Aren't we lucky! Sean is giving us a strip tease!" Still, the drivers appeared untroubled about the prospects for an unsuccessful Tortoise trip. It was only the second day and there were many more surprises in store.

Lingering Suspicions

While the drivers studiously ignored the tension created by their insouciance, some passengers attempted hesitantly to do likewise. Indeed, most of the male passengers tended to feel less threatened by the drivers. An illustrator from Canada named Hal, said he thought all the sex-talk was "just a way of getting to know each other."

9

The drivers' articulated reasons for conspiring against inhibitions were often superficially non-voyeuristic. Time and time again, Curt and Arthur emphasized their primary objective was to be "cool." In addition to being more tolerant of nudity and sex, "being cool" implied that one should not fret—as uptight travelers generally do—about schedules, routes and destinations. The drivers typical responses to queries about the itinerary were: "Are you happy with where you're at? If you are, then relax and enjoy yourself. If not, how will going to some other place solve your problem?" Rebuffs such as these tended to preempt vocalized concerns about the itinerary.

However, the same logic did not easily transpose to nudity and sex. Many of the women were, to say the least, dubious about the drivers' lofty aspirations. Maggie, a female passenger, repeatedly declared "All you want is to see us naked!" One of the tiresome facts of life for women—from which the Tortoise offered no respite—is that they are pursued relentlessly as sexual objects. Although, with an effort, one could read altruism into the drivers' attitudes (i.e., "lose your inhibitions and be happy"), their communiqués generally sounded more like cheesy come-ons. Thus, it was not difficult to fathom Maggie's skepticism. A woman named Bernice added quizzically, "Why do we have to be naked to have fun?"

Thus, throughout the early days of our journey the drivers thwarted the development of a "mobile utopia" (McGettigan, 1999a) because of their curious, aggressive, and irritating demands. Predictably, onboard tension persisted and the passengers remained exceedingly boundary-conscious. I felt, once again, that maintaining a problematically balanced analytical perspective was child's play. The more relentless the drivers were, the more fiercely passengers clung to countervailing suspicions.

Consolidating Disapproval

Midway through week one a pocket of antagonized female passengers coalesced. The "disapproving group" often stood out by whispering in tightly closed circles. Members of this group also announced regularly "I don't shit or shag in public!" The disapprovers also voiced judgmental comments about the deportment of both drivers and other passengers: "I can't stand it when women don't shave! Look at that tan line! Is Curt swimming without his shorts again?!"

On the fourth day, we arrived at Big Bend National Park and spent the morning hiking. After lunch, we stopped in Terlingua, a Texas frontier town, and then drove to a remote, brush-filled state park. Curt parked the bus in the prime site, only thirty meters from the Rio Grande, and announced that we were spending the night. While a cloud of dust settled, Curt also recommended a swim in the Rio Grande. Being late in a very warm afternoon, the idea of a cool rinse sounded unusually agreeable. Most of the passengers changed into their swimming suits, while the drivers stepped straight into the river after dropping their shorts.

I took a beer from the cooler and stood on the riverbank. The Rio Grande was chalky and surprisingly narrow; I judged that I could skip a flat stone across it with ease. Upstream Hal tiptoed in and then plunged into the swift stream. When he waded out on the far side, Hal became the first among us to set foot in Mexico. Inspired by Hal's humble achievement, a flood of swimmers surged to Mexico.

After finishing my beer, I walked to the point where Hal had launched. The smooth stones wiggled underfoot as I splashed into the silty water. I dove and then pulled hard through the river's strong current. When the stream slackened I lifted my head and was struck by a glob of mud. For the next twenty minutes, mud flew wildly and the air filled with a rich, earthy fragrance. While, for the most part, the mud battle served as a harmless, tension-relieving game, there were several casualties: Sean was struck in the left eye, and Sandra, normally a cheerful Swiss woman, suffered a direct hit in the mouth.

Just as the mud battle was beginning to subside, Arthur noticed that Maggie, Carla, and Leslie (three principal members of the disapproving group) had crossed the river but were standing beyond the range of battle. With a piercing shriek, Arthur charged out of the water and sprinted after the women. While she ran, Leslie roared, "Keep away from me, you dirty, naked, disgusting hippie!" As Arthur streaked after his prey, I was struck by the aptness of this image. The more that Arthur and Curt pressed their agenda, the more they incited fear, rejection, and disgust among their targets. Perhaps Hobbes (1996) was right in claiming that, minus strict social constraints, we might all become howling, lascivious werewolves like Arthur.

Photo 4: Big Bend Camp Site

Following the mud battle most of the former combatants got together for a beer. Interestingly, as the atmosphere became more chummy, the disapproving group became more physically and socially reclusive. Hal shot me a puzzled look after spotting the solitary clique and asked "Why did they come on the Tortoise?"

At the time, I shared Hal's perplexity. I sympathized with the disapproving group, however, my goal was to observe *evolving* group dynamics on the Tortoise—and it appeared as though the disapprovers were holding up the process. Impatiently, I thought that if the disapprovers would just relax, they might do us the courtesy of permitting "more important"

11

developments to unfold. Although I had not tried this line of argument on the disapproving group, others had—but to no avail. The disapprovers were far too suspicious to be budged by argument. In fact, the more compelling the argument, the more their suspicions were aroused.

Nevertheless, over the course of the next twenty-four hours, the disapprovers' attitudes finally yielded. Interestingly, however, this turnabout was produced by neither argument nor appeal. Rather, their transformation was produced by charm: the irresistible charm of the Green Tortoise.

The Irresistible Charm of the Green Tortoise

During our camp out there was a pronounced party atmosphere. This was due in part to the mud battle, but also because of the next day's plans. In the morning we were traveling to Boquillas, a small Mexican village. This was a much anticipated day because of the international border crossing and because of Mexico's tariff-free liquor.

Following a quick breakfast of cold cereal and juice, we rambled for an hour along an isolated road and then turned into a well-hidden parking area. Before opening the front door, Curt reminded us that Boquillas was an unusual tourist destination. He urged us to respect the town for what it was: a real Mexican village.

Photo 5: Boquillas

Although there was only one trail out of the parking lot, a group of men sitting on folding chairs herded passersby toward the river saying, "Amigo, amigo. The river is this way." The footpath was narrow, well-trodden, and shaded by tall trees. At the riverbank, a Mexican man busily loaded people into a rowboat. When its seats were full, the boatman hurriedly pushed the craft into the current. There were two oars in the boat, and I was annoyed when Jake, a perpetually drunken "free-rider," refused the boatman's request for assistance. The boatman had to tug hard through the current. On the far side, a man stood quietly by a pick-up truck, and as his customers scrambled ashore, the boatman directed them to pay the "nice man" two dollars: one for the trip they had just taken and another for their return. They paid their fares and wandered across a wide beach covered with large, round stones.

The boatman wasted no time in shooting back across the river. We refilled the boat and then Sean helped paddle through the current. After landing we followed the established routine: paying the boatman's partner and then picking up the trail to Boquillas. At the outskirts of the village, the trail swung uphill past a line of shacks. Animals were tied outside many of the little shanties, and, occasionally, children would burst out waving wristbands and necklaces. Atop the hill, there were two relatively large buildings: an unpopulated market and a bar.

I asked Hal if I could buy him a drink, and he agreed obligingly. The bar was a white-washed, flat-roofed building with royal blue trim. The door stood open as did each of the deep-set, adobe windows. The interior was simply a large room with a wood counter running along the side wall. Inside the door, a guitarist sat on a stool and crooned loud, unmelodious songs. Tables took up much of the bar's central space, while the rear was reserved for two dilapidated pool tables.

I bought two bottles of Carta Blanca and sat down with Hal. In a short time, Perry, a dark-skinned English traveler, invited us to a game of pool. The game progressed slowly because the table's surface played like a sandbox. In the middle of our game, I noticed that Jake had acquired a bottle of tequila. His bottle of Cuervo Gold quickly attracted an enlarging, boisterous throng.

Hal and I lost our pool game, but rather than joining the others, I sat on the unused pool table and observed the tequila party. It was fascinating to witness how eagerly the tequila drinkers discarded their formerly inviolate inhibitions, and it occurred to me that the tequila appeared to produce a "slingshot effect." The drivers had been challenging people to become intimate in a very short span of time. While the passengers had resisted the drivers' provocations, these counter-pressures had elevated rather than diffused tension. However, the passengers' defiance had risen to the challenge until, in the impersonal atmosphere of the bar, they let their emotions explode. With the assistance of an acceptable vehicle—tequila—a wave of tolerance burst over the drinkers like a tsunami. Their opposition had only tightened the springs of the snare.

I was feeling rather pleased with myself as I watched the mounting uproar—much as Thorne (1979) must have when she wrote:

> ...I sensed...that I could have my cake and eat it too. I could share in the excitement, the thrills of participating in events that seemed almost magnetic—and be spared the costs: the uncertainty of risk-taking (Thorne, 1979, p. 81).

I noted smugly that even though I was accepted as a member of the group, I could still control the intoxication of both the alcohol and the Tortoise. I alone remained in charge of my distant and privileged viewpoint.

13

The besotted passengers were not content to sit and drink, they also began dancing. At first they capered amongst themselves, but soon they began partnering with village residents. I presume such antics were a routine spectacle for the inhabitants of Boquillas, however, I noted surprise when Judy, a small Irish woman, began squirting the locals with water. From that point on, the drunken scene in the bar became utterly outrageous. Many passengers had guzzled so much tequila that they were having trouble walking. Others slowly slid down the walls they were leaning on, or out of the chairs they could no longer sit in. As a viscous torpor of grievous intoxication descended upon the partiers, Hal borrowed the guitarist's six-string and began playing "A Whole Lotta' Shakin'." While Hal jammed, several others began stacking a column of beer bottles. The pillar climbed to four feet before all the bottles crashed to the floor.

Even though I was pleased to witness such a momentous change in group dynamics, the ear-splitting clatter of the bottles also made me anxious. The drunkards had reached the point where a bit of gentle supervision was advisable. Although I was not unwilling to aid my intemperate companions, it was not my desire to take charge. I wanted to participate in the flow of events as "one of the gang," instead of imposing restrictions that would alter the natural course of events. However, before impending disaster could strike, the drivers appeared. Thus, I was spared the trouble—for a little while longer—of having to muddle my role as a problematically-balanced observer.

A Double-Edged Sword

Impressed as they were by their charges' stupefaction, the drivers were not intent on concluding the party. Instead, they were even convinced to join some of the fun. For example, Maggie announced that she wished to have a special tequila shot with Arthur. To my lasting amazement, Maggie poured a whopping shot of tequila into Arthur's mouth and then sucked out the liquor with a horribly sloppy kiss. As a circle of onlookers groaned in disgust, I inwardly rejoiced. Repulsive as this display might have been, a truce had been achieved. Now that even the most disapproving of passengers had embraced the drivers—symbolized by the revolting tequila kiss—I suddenly became more optimistic about the potential development of a mobile utopia (McGettigan, 1999a).

Indeed, the passengers had undergone a remarkable shift in their relationship to the drivers. Prior to Boquillas, the passengers had resisted the drivers' attempts to explode inhibitions, whereas now they needed to rely upon the drivers to temper their lunatic escapades. While the drivers' introduced a calming influence, there were soon additional crises. Two normally peaceful men, named Frederick and Peter, got into a shoving match. After Frederick threw Peter to the floor twice, Curt intervened and then signaled to the door.

The drivers made arrangements with several truck owners to provide transport to the river. Following a bumpy ride along the dusty trail, the Rio Grande presented the next major stumbling block. I volunteered to help row the first boat across the river. In the confident hands of the experienced boatman, our navigation was flawless. However, the process of disembarking presented additional difficulties.

The boat landing was nothing more than the muddy riverbank. Getting a sure footing on the slippery mud was difficult enough for the relatively sober, but almost impossible for the inebriated. I threw my backpack to the top of the bank and then, with Sean's help, hoisted the

14

first load of partiers ashore. When finished, Sean and I looked at the befuddled state of the next boatload and decided to assist them, too.

Before the final shuttle, Curt and Arthur put their clothes in the boat and swam across the river. The drivers had not bothered to pay for a ride earlier, however, Frederick and Monty, a staggeringly intoxicated Englishman, decided they too should swim. The four skinny-dippers plunged into the river. While one crossing was sufficient for the rest, Frederick took an extra lap. Upon his return, Arthur urged Frederick to climb ashore. Monty, on the other hand, had departed jovially without his clothing—I heard bawdy cheers from the direction of the bus when, I presumed, Monty hove into view.

The final boat crossed the river and, with the drivers in the lead, we returned to the bus. As we reassembled, the partiers' high spirits renewed. Monty had not yet bothered to put on his clothes and, rather than censure, his performance elicited howls of encouragement from unqualified admirers.

Although I was hoping for rest, a head count soon determined that two people were missing. No one had seen Jake or a female passenger, Amanda, cross the river. Since few others were steady on their feet, Sean and I volunteered to conduct a search. In the quiet, away from the mayhem, my head hummed like a tuning fork.

Before I could grow used to the tranquility, Sean and I heard shrieks coming from the river. We decided to speed our pace and, at the landing site, were puzzled to find neither the boat nor its operator. However, we were shaken from our perplexity by an angry bellow. The boatman, who was lying in the water about thirty feet downstream, exclaimed "It's not right! You shouldn't have left me with a crazy man!" I stood frozen in bewilderment, but the boatman pointed to Jake, who clung to tree roots as he scaled the riverbank. I shouted, "Jake, what the hell are you doing?" He ignored me, but the boatman explained that Jake had pitched he and Amanda out of the boat. "It's not right. He's got no respect. Now my boat is gone!" I was too stunned to respond. However, I was jolted out of my shock when the boatman added that Amanda was still in the river.

I darted to the end of a small point. Unable to spot Amanda, I decided to jump into the river. I was much too alarmed to ponder the methodological implications of helping Amanda (i.e., Would my interference contaminate the field site irreparably? What happens when an audience-member interferes in a performance?). In urgent situations, even the most fastidious researchers have foregone scientific constraints. For example, Wax (1971) stated after joining the resistance against a terrorist gang:

> If anyone had told me that I was about to "interfere" in a field situation and that I was thereby breaking a primary rule of scientific procedure, I think I would have laughed or, perhaps, told the admonisher to go to hell (Wax, 1971, p. 158).

I took off my shirt, but, in my haste, forgot about my glasses. A moment after I dove into the river, I realized that my glasses were lost and unrecoverable. I swam into the central current and searched from bank to bank. It was not until I had rounded a bend that I sighted the boat. A Mexican man wearing only white underpants was standing in it. He was struggling to control the spinning vessel, and, in a swirl of backwater, I finally spotted Amanda. She was trying to grab a rope, but the boat's unsteady rocking yanked the line from her hand. As I drew closer, I encouraged Amanda to swim to the Mexican riverbank. We were only a few feet from calmer, shallower water, but Amanda failed to understand. Instead, she lunged for the boat and gagged on a mouthful of water. I urged her anxiously to concentrate on swimming to shore.

When I managed to gather her attention, we agreed to swim sidestroke, facing each other, to the Mexican bank. With a few steady, purposeful strokes, I was able to stand and help Amanda to the beach. The man who had rescued the boat was also ashore, and in the process of hauling the boat upstream. When Amanda had her breath, we turned toward the landing site. As we walked along the rocky shore, Amanda puzzled over what had happened. She said she remembered that one moment everything was fine, and, an instant later, she was foundering in the water.

At the landing, the boatman appeared annoyed with Amanda. On the far side, Curt, Sean, and a few others had collected atop the bank. The moment we docked, there was a flurry of questions. The boatman explained that the accident came about after Jake made crude sexual advances toward Amanda. When she resisted, the boatman intervened and Jake dumped them both into the river. Jake had completed the crossing and then cast the boat adrift.

At the bus, Curt called sternly for Jake. He emerged looking like a puppy who had pooped on the carpet. Curt asked Jake to explain what happened at the river, and, without lifting his eyes, Jake shrugged and said, "I don't know. I think someone might have fallen out of the boat." The boatman blurted out, "That's not true! He jumped the girl and then threw us both in the water." Faced with contradictory stories, Curt turned to Amanda. She shook her head slowly and responded that she had no idea what had happened. Given the lack of other available witnesses, Curt chose to drop the matter.

Although Curt believed that there was no point in pursuing the inquiry, I felt differently. Even if events had not transpired precisely as the boatman described, I felt sure that Jake must have been more culpable. I looked at Jake and spat, "You deserve to be in prison!" Jake was rattled by my denunciation, and he strode toward me saying, "You can't prove anything!" Curt stood in his way and then asked if I had witnessed anything. Since I had only observed the aftermath, I had to shake my head. Curt admonished me: "Look man, if you didn't see anything, you can't say anything." Bitterly, I conceded, but fumed in exasperation.

The boatman resignedly informed Curt that he felt entitled to reparations. Curt sighed, reached into his pocket, and said, "Look, I've got twenty bucks on me." The boatman accepted the money and then asked Curt to deliver two new oars. I returned to the bus and sat on a bench. Amanda wandered to the rear platform with Jake. They appeared intent on working out their differences. I was too frazzled to caution Amanda against further involvement with Jake. Instead, I draped a towel over my head and rubbed my eyes. As I did so, Hal said, "Hey! Where are your glasses?" I shook my head and told him they were in the river. He gaped in alarm, but I raised my hands to forestall further discussion.

Demolished Roles and Restructured Perception

Curt drove out of the parking lot, but rather than returning to the main road, he diverged onto another dirt lane. After wrestling the bus along a series of dusty paths, he pulled off and shut down the engine. One mile down a nearby path, Curt claimed, there was an old historic hot springs. While others rushed off in search of the springs, I scanned the desert for a likely retreat.

In the early dusk, I took few steps into the scrubby landscape and plumped down, hidden and alone, on the crunchy husk of a dead plant.

In the quiet desert, my mind raged. Chief among my thoughts emerged an overriding antipathy for Jake. Even though I am not usually an advocate of imprisonment—I like to imagine that there must be more constructive ways of managing troublesome people—I felt as though Jake deserved incarceration; he deserved to be handled as inhumanely as he had treated others. Also, I was still annoyed that Jake had been permitted back on the bus. I seriously considered deserting in protest.

It is not unheard of for researchers to "loathe" (Lofland and Lofland, 1984) some of people they study. However, despite the enmity that I bore for Jake[1], I decided that it would only compound the day's injustices if I permitted him to disrupt my work. Therefore, I decided not to abandon my research project, however, I was forced to radically revamp my perception of the Tortoise. That is, from the outset, I had cultivated the ludicrous misperception that while I may have been physically present on the bus, my analytical psyche had been removed—as if I had been a researcher "witnessing a reality impervious to his presence" (Pollner and Emerson 1983, p. 236). However, the river incident convinced me that no one had been acting—especially for my benefit—and I had not been in an audience. Furthermore, I had developed the unshakable conviction that I had both the right and responsibility to interfere with trouble-makers. To put it mildly, I was disgusted with my naïve orienting assumptions and I was disenchanted with the Green Tortoise.

As a result, I found myself in a quandary. I could no longer tolerate either of the available realities: either to continue in the role of "a good researcher" or to become an actor in the "Tortoise drama." Instead, I decided to proceed without a predetermined set of anchoring assumptions.

Back on Board

The afternoon in Boquillas had produced the desired effect on many of the passengers. The shouts of cavorting bathers echoed throughout the surrounding hills. When I rejoined the others, I found the hot springs full of noisy, nudists. Again, I had to marvel at the results of their binge. The sobering crowd appeared perfectly comfortable about skinny dipping together. Yet, although I had sidestepped the drunken insanity in Boquillas, I no longer sensed I was the master of my surroundings. I felt dizzy and slightly aswirl, as though I were caught in an unseen current.

In the days that followed, I noted with interest a new twist in my behavior. After

---

[1]   I decided that my opinion of Jake could not improve sufficiently to tolerate any kind of interaction with him. Instead I decided to do my best to ignore him. While this was a daunting project because of our restricted quarters, nevertheless, we were both able to maintain an impressive distance for the remainder of the trip.

Interestingly, as reprehensible as I consider Jake's behavior, I found his presence instructive. Largely because of my abhorrence, I consciously—and not without annoying plagues of conscience—exercised double standards in relation to his behavior. Thus, I learned useful lessons about the value-based nature of my "objective," analytical mind.

Boquillas, I became more outspoken about the potential dangers of various activities. I had no desire to witness any more disasters—no matter how sociologically interesting. When Chagnon (1977) encountered a Yanomamö mother who was starving her daughter he was faced with a dilemma. Although this sort of mistreatment was not negatively sanctioned among the Yanomamö, Chagnon's culturally-biased sense of morality compelled him to intervene. Chagnon imposed an alien morality—and, in doing so, altered the "natural" course of events—because he could not condone such brutal neglect. While Chagnon's culturally-biased intrusion threatened the validity of his research, in another sense he also enhanced its validity.

Fleuhr-Lobban (1995) argues that social scientists do a disservice by avoiding interference in the plight of the oppressed. By adhering to a "holy" (Kvale 1995) orientation to science, researchers minimize contamination, but also acquiesce to forms of coercion that systematically subvert truth, e.g., interpreting quietude as consensus (Gaventa, 1982). Although Fleuhr-Lobban is cognizant of the dangers associated with superimposing alien cultural standards, she argues that science cannot ignore the misfortunes of the oppressed while also esteeming truth. Thus, Fleuhr-Lobban proposes that truth-seeking must be associated with the amelioration of particular injustices within and across cultural boundaries.

Truth on the Green Tortoise

After Boquillas, my interference, much like Chagnon's, at times approximated surrogate parenthood. For example, during a day in New Orleans, one woman replied "Yes, Daddy!" when I cautioned her against the hazards of the French Quarter. These solicitations eventually earned me the nickname, "the father of the bus." Nevertheless, rather than contaminating the Tortoise, my morally-involved participation affirmed and advanced its "naturally" evolving social dynamics. That is, after Boquillas there was also another notable modification in my behavior: I became increasingly caught up in the enthusiasm of the adventure trip. For example, if somebody sprayed me with water, I would spray twice as much back. Also, during a food fight, I found myself hurling more muck when everyone else had given up the game. A man named Ken, who was thunderstruck by my antics, remarked repeatedly about how much I had changed *since I lost my glasses*.

Photo 6: Tidying Up

Although it was not clear at the time, when I rejected the perspective that had characterized other passengers as actors, I began to treat the Tortoise as a real place. As a result, I became more susceptible to the "Tortoise Effect." That is, I began associating with others in the zany fashion the Tortoise inspires because my inhibitions had gone out the window behind theirs. By breaking through the boundaries that had preserved my aloofness, I was "charmed" by the Tortoise and drawn to a more verisimilar (Lincoln and Denzin, 1994) understanding of its unique experience.

Conclusion

The social world is far too complex for imperfect scientists ever to presume that they have determined its final truths. Yet, although ultimate truths may be forever out of reach, humans are still capable of changing profoundly "the shape of the thinkable" (Gordon, 1991, p.8). As certain as we my be about "absolute truths," the process of redefining reality (McGettigan, 1998a, 1999a, 1999b, 2000) generally causes such certainties to appear, in a new light, as rather silly beliefs (e.g., the earth being flat, or lying at the center of the universe). Therefore, I assert that scientific truth is best conceived as a vehicle to transport inquiry toward "the continent of thought just beyond the horizon" (Pefanis, 1991, p. 138). At any rate, I believe that imperfect scientists can most faithfully serve truth by caring more about people than knowledge.

"Good science" has been criticized repeatedly for maintaining established paradigms (Kuhn, 1970; Lather, 1995; Lemert, 1991, 1999; Wright, 1992) more effectively than divining truth. If truth emerges through the process of reducing distortions over knowledge (Habermas, 1981; Lemert, 1991; McGettigan, 1998a, 1999a, 2000), then a sacred (Kvale, 1995) view of scientific validity obviates truth by endorsing a wide range of sacrosanct limitations on knowledge. As in the early stages of my Tortoise journey, such constraints tend to insulate and filter "good scientific" perceptions. Yet, when I "botched" my project (i.e., when I lost my glasses, contaminated the field site, and muddled my good scientific perspective) I acquired more and better information about the Green Tortoise than I ever could have otherwise. Thus, I argue that truth-seekers would be better off caring about people more than "good science" because, at the very least, privileging human welfare decreases the chances that imperfect researchers will inflict harm. At best, caring more about people will help advance the cause of justice by challenging the subtle, diabolical, and often unintended forms of power that, in turn, limit the production of truth within and across societies.

References

Belgrave, Linda Liska, and Kenneth J. Smith, 1995. "Negotiated Validity in Collaborative Ethnography." *Qualitative Inquiry* 1: (1) 69-86.

Chagnon, Napoleon A., 1977. *Yanomamö: The Fierce People*. 2d ed. New York: Holt, Rinehart and Winston.

Dahl, Robert A., 1957. "The Concept of Power." *Behavioural Science* 2: 201-205.

Denzin, Norman K., 1994. "The Art and Politics of Interpretation." Pp. 500-515 in *Handbook of Qualitative Research*. Norman K. Denzin and Yvonna S. Lincoln (Eds.). Thousand Oaks: Sage.

Douglas, Jack D., 1976. *Investigative Social Research: Individual and Team Field Research*. Beverly Hills: Sage.

Emerson, Robert M., ed., 1983. *Contemporary Field Research: A Collection of Readings*. Prospect Heights, Ill: Waveland Press, Inc.

Evans-Pritchard, E. E., 1940. The Nuer. Oxford: Clarendon Press.

Fleuhr-Lobban, Carolyn, 1995. "Cultural Relativism and Universal Rights." *The Chronicle of Higher Education*. 41: 39 (June 9) B1-B2.

Gaventa, John, 1982. *Power and Powerlessness: Quiescence and Rebellion in an Appalachian Valley*. Urbana: University of Illinois Press.

Gold, Raymond L., 1958. "Roles in Sociological Field Observations." *Social Forces* 36: 217-

223.

Habermas, Jürgen, 1981. *Theory of Communicative Action.* London: Heinemann.

Hobbes, Thomas, 1996. *Leviathan.* Cambridge: Cambridge University Press.

Kanter, Rosabeth Moss, 1972. *Commitment and Community: Communes and Utopias in Sociological Perspective.* Cambridge: Harvard University Press.

Kuhn, Thomas S., 1970. *The Structure of Scientific Revolutions.* Chicago: University of Chicago Press.

Kvale, Steinar, 1995. "The Social Construction of Validity." *Qualitative Inquiry* 1: (1) 19-40.

Lather, Patti A. 1995. "The Validity of Angels: Interpretive and Textual Strategies in Researching the Lives of Women With HIV/AIDS." *Qualitative Inquiry* 1: (1) 41-68.

Lemert, Charles, 1991. "The End of Ideology, Really." *Sociological Theory* 9: 2 (Fall) 164-172.

Lemert, Charles (Ed.), 1999. *Social Theory: The Multicultural and Classic Readings.* Boulder, CO: Westview.

Lincoln, Yvonna S. and Norman K. Denzin, 1994. "The Fifth Moment." Pp. 575-586 in *Handbook of Qualitative Research.* Norman K. Denzin and Yvonna S. Lincoln (Eds.). Thousand Oaks: Sage.

Lofland, John and Lyn H. Lofland, 1984. *Analyzing Social Settings: A Guide to Qualitative Observation and Analysis.* 2d ed. Belmont, CA.: Wadsworth.

Malinowski, Bronislaw, 1967. *A Diary in the Strict Sense of the Term.* New York: Harcourt, Brace and World.

McGettigan, 1997. "Uncorrected Insight: Metaphor and Transcendence 'After Truth' in Qualitative Inquiry." Published in *Qualitative Inquiry* 3 (3): 366-383.

McGettigan, Timothy, 1998a. "Redefining Reality: Epiphany as a Standard of Postmodern Truth." *Electronic Journal of Sociology* 3 (4). http://www.sociology.org/vol003.004/mcgettigan.article.1998.html

McGettigan, Timothy, 1998b. "Reflections in an Unblinking Eye: Negotiating the Representation of Postmodern Identities in the Production of a Documentary." *Sociological Research Online* 3 (1). http://www.socresonline.org.uk/3/1/7.html

McGettigan, Timothy, 1999a. *Utopia on Wheels: Blundering Down the Road to Reality.* Lanham, MD.: University Press of America.

McGettigan, Timothy, 1999b. "Editor's Introduction." Published in *Theory and Science* 1 (1). http://theoryandscience.icaap.org/content/vol001.001/Editors_Intro.html

McGettigan, Timothy, 2000. "Flawed by Design: The Virtues and Limitations of Postmodern Theory." Published in *Theory & Science* 1 (1). http://theoryandscience.icaap.org/content/vol001.001/05mcgettigan.html

Mead, Margaret, ed., 1966. *Writings of Ruth Benedict: An Anthropologist at Work.* New York: Atherton Press.

Neumann, Mark, 1993. "Living on Tortoise Time: Alternative Travel as the Pursuit of Lifestyle." *Symbolic Interaction* 16: (3) 201-235.

Pollner, Melvin and Robert M. Emerson, 1983. "The Dynamics of Inclusion and Distance in Fieldwork Relations." In *Contemporary Field Research: A Collection of Readings.* (Robert M. Emerson, ed.) Prospect Heights, Ill.: Waveland Press, Inc.

Richardson, Laurel, 1994. "Writing: A Method of Inquiry." Pp. 516-529 in *Handbook of Qualitative Research.* Norman K. Denzin and Yvonna S. Lincoln (Eds.). Thousand Oaks: Sage.

Rothschild-Whitt, Joyce, 1979. "The Collectivist Organization: An Alternative to Rational-Bureaucratic Models." *American Sociological Review* 44: (August) 509-527.

Seidman, Steven, 1991. "The End of Sociological Theory: The Postmodern Hope." *Sociological Theory* 9: 2 (Fall) 131-146.

Thorne, Barrie, 1979. "Political Activist as Participant Observer: Conflicts of Commitment in a Study of the Draft Resistance Movement of the 1960's." *Symbolic Interaction* 2: 73-88.

Wax, Rosalie H., 1971. *Doing Fieldwork: Warnings and Advice.* Chicago: University of

Chicago Press.

Wichroski, Mary Anne, 1996. "Breaking Silence: Some Fieldwork Strategies in Cloistered and Non-Cloistered Communities." *Qualitative Sociology* (19) 1: 153-170.

Wolfe, Tom, 1968. *The Electric Kool-Aid Acid Test*. New York: Farrar, Strauss and Giroux.

Wright, Will, 1992. *Wild Knowledge: Science, Language, and Social Life in a Fragile Environment*. Minneapolis: University of Minnesota Press.

CHAPTER TWO

Reflections in an Unblinking Eye[1]

Negotiating Identity in the Production of a Documentary

Abstract

The presence of a motion picture documentary team during a Green Tortoise adventure trip created a variety of unique opportunities to evaluate the construction of identity in a postmodern, "cinematic society" (Denzin, 1995). While, the "gaze" (Nichols, 1991) of cameras often participated directly in the production of "spectacular" events, the "simulating" (Baudrillard, 1988, 1994) gaze of the cameras also served as a "reflexive mechanism" through which to expose cinematic influences that construct contemporary reality.

Field Research on the Green Tortoise

In July of 1994, as part of a research project in which I examined the evolving frameworks of power in contemporary society, I took an eleven-day, New York City to San Francisco, adventure trip on the Green Tortoise. The Green Tortoise is a bus travel company, based in San Francisco, that emerged from the rebellious youth countercultures of the 1960's. The philosophy of the Green Tortoise (e.g., "Arrive inspired, not dog tired") is to transform traveling from a misery into an adventure. This goal is achieved in part by converting their bus interiors into an unrestricted lounging space filled with cushioned benches, tables and platforms. Also, whereas conventional travel may often be characterized as "being alone in a crowd" (Riesman, 1950), the open arrangement of the Tortoise's interior space practically compels one to associate with others as one travels. Last but not least, the Tortoise also carries its own food and kitchen. Thus, although its amenities may be a bit rustic, the Green Tortoise attends assiduously to a wide variety of desirable creature comforts.

Video Clip #1: www.socresonline.org.uk/3/1/video/vid1qt.html

I chose to do a series of field research projects on the Green Tortoise because I wished to explore the structure of a particular type of counterculture. Since the 1960's a variety of businesses have attempted to strike a tenuous compromise between a philosophical rejection of mainstream culture and organizational viability (Rothschild-Whitt, 1979). The Green Tortoise

---

[1]   This is an updated version of an article originally published in *Sociological Research Online*: http://www.socresonline.org.uk/3/1/7.html

is an excellent example of just such a countercultural organization. Travel on the Green Tortoise is based on a commune-like atmosphere (i.e., communal sitting, sleeping, and eating arrangements), but Tortoise-travel is also conventional due to its inescapable reliance upon fossil fuel-guzzling buses that are driven on asphalt roads by licensed drivers, etc. Thus, the Green Tortoise is clearly dependent upon contemporary society, but its orientation towards the unconventional also typifies a compromised rejection of the mainstream. I wanted to get "inside of the shell" of this type of organization because I wished to observe the dynamic processes involved in incorporating countercultural philosophical practices into conventional organizational settings. I wanted to see if these organizations were able to generate internal "spaces" that were any different than the conventional world they had, in part, disavowed. Could such conventionally-viable organizations actually originate realistic countercultural challenges to mainstream society?

A New Twist on a Familiar Adventure

Shortly after I had made travel arrangements for my second cross-country adventure trip on the Green Tortoise,[1] I received a letter from a film producer, named Debra,[2] who was in charge of Diem Productions, a New York-based, independent film company. In the letter, Debra explained that she had made arrangements to shoot a documentary on the July, 1994 westbound Green Tortoise cross-country trip. Debra acknowledged that while she intended for her documentary to capture the "natural" events on the Tortoise trip, she was also aware that she and her crew were going to comprise an unusual intrusion. Nevertheless, she believed that her filming of the documentary could actually enhance the spirit of adventure on this Green Tortoise journey.

> I would like to say at the outset that we are not going to be invasive and if you do not want to participate, we will not force you...We hope that our filming of this trip will make it an experience above and beyond what you expected when you first signed up (Excerpt from Debra's introductory letter).

Indeed, I felt confident that Debra's optimistic forecast would prove to be prophetic. I could imagine that the presence of the documentary team would precipitate an interesting range of "reactive" effects (Becker, 1986; Denzin, 1989a; Smith, et al., 1975) in the passengers. In addition, I also sensed that my interactions with the camera crew would produce a fascinating reflexive puzzle: in the course of my own "voyeuristic" (Denzin, 1995) observation project, I would be observing "voyeuristically" the activities of other voyeurs as they were engaged in the process of observing the people that I was observing—and, of course, numbering amongst the "observed" would be *myself*. Thus, much as one's visible reflections are multiplied by positioning mirrors closely together, the presence of the camera crew's "gaze" would augment substantially the number of reflective "angles" through which the events of our adventure trip

---

[1]   This was my third trip on the Green Tortoise. The first was a weeklong round trip on the north/south commuter that runs between Seattle and Los Angeles. The second trip was an eastbound cross-country adventure trip in October of 1993 from San Francisco to New York.

[2]   Except for mine and my wife's, I have substituted pseudonyms for all personal names in this article.

might be analyzed. Therefore, while I resolved to remain acutely aware of the reactive effects that the camera crew's gaze had upon the westbound adventure, I was also determined to monitor closely the impact of the camera's gaze upon my own thoughts and actions.

My second cross-country adventure trip on the Green Tortoise began in New York City on Sunday, July 17, 1994. I was accompanied by my wife, Susan, who was embarking on her first Green Tortoise trip. We rendezvoused with the bus in upper Manhattan next to the George Washington Street Bus Station. The Green Tortoise and its passengers appeared out of place in the dense, urban environment: in the glowing haze at the end of a hot summer day a disorganized crowd of people—with camera operators in their midst—lingered on the sidewalk next to a travel-weary, green bus.

There was a small, white van parked behind the Tortoise. The film crew needed to bring along too much equipment (e.g., cameras, sound recorders, film, etc.) to carry it on the bus. In total, there were five members of the film crew: Debra and her co-producer, Amy, two camera operators, named Ken and James, and one camera operator/van driver, named Chuck. As we were being filmed by squinting men with portable cameras on their shoulders, I almost forgot the routine of getting loaded onto the bus. One of the drivers, the "lead" driver named Jeff, was preoccupied with the task of getting off the streets of New York. Thus, before Susan and I had even paid for our tickets, Jeff asked us to board the bus to speed our escape from the city. When he had driven about ten miles south, Jeff stopped at a roadside pullout and, there, finally calmed down. As we sat in the grass eating freshly baked Italian cookies, Jeff explained his philosophy as a Tortoise driver.

Jeff's attitude towards running the bus was different than that of other drivers. First of all, Jeff did not allow drinking on the bus when he was driving—this is not the usual policy on Tortoise adventure trips.[1] Jeff also enumerated a number of policies that appeared to be geared towards making his passengers' transition to life on the Tortoise relatively gentle (e.g., he would stop for restroom breaks any time[2] and, incredibly, he would try to maintain an itinerary). Jeff acknowledged that some of his policies were different than the norm for Tortoise drivers. Thus, he added that he would need the film crew—who were filming at the time—to edit some of the things that he had said in order to protect his job. I thought this was a curious "problem" for Jeff to have. Whereas it was against the law for people to drink alcohol on the bus, the documentary could provide the kind of evidence that might land Jeff in trouble with his employer for having overly "uptight" policies. At the same time, another thought entered my mind. Although Jeff did not appear out of place on the Tortoise, I could imagine that his law-abiding policies and his accommodating attitude might project the kind of image that would minimize negative publicity for the Tortoise.

After our orientation, we got back on the bus. Jeff wanted to drive further that evening before performing "the miracle." "The miracle" is the process through which Tortoise buses are transformed into sleeper-coaches. There is nothing especially "miraculous" about these transformations, however, it does require an enormous amount of reorganization to create

---

[1]   Later, a male passenger, named Harvey, told me that on a previous Tortoise trip—an adventure during which he claimed to have consumed "a twenty-four pack of beer a day for seven days straight"—he had heard about one Tortoise driver who did not allow drinking on his bus. He added jokingly, "Wouldn't it be my bloody luck to end up on this bus!"

[2]   Tortoise buses have no onboard toilet facilities.

enough interior space to stretch out thirty-five sleeping bags. Jeff stopped the bus to perform the miracle at a truck stop on I-80 in Pennsylvania. Once again, Jeff threw himself into this labor with vigor—practically accomplishing the entire task by himself. When the transformation was completed, we packed into the bus like sardines and then jostled through the night in a haze of semi-sleep.

The Influences of Different Gazes

The morning dawned bright and early. It is difficult to sleep late on the Tortoise because the breaking sunlight sears relentlessly through the bus's many side windows. Soon after crossing into Indiana Jeff exited the freeway and found a state park where we could make breakfast. At the park, Jeff set to work immediately on the production of breakfast, whereas just about everyone else went for a swim in a nearby lake. It was a cool morning, so most of the swimmers were out of the water quickly. Since, for me, the worst part of swimming in cold water is the initial shock, once I was in the water I decided to linger. My extended swim provided an opportunity to become acquainted with the other two remaining swimmers, Daniel and Mark. Mark was a vacationing arts columnist and Daniel was in the midst of a "pause" in his life during which he was traveling to California to find out where _he_ was. I was puzzled to find that neither Mark nor Daniel registered any alarm when I told them that I was engaged in a research project.

On previous Green Tortoise trips, when I had explained to other passengers that I was conducting a research project, they generally responded with wide-eyed amazement and said things like: "You mean you're doing research _right now_? On _this_? On _us_? On _me_?!" Thus, I had anticipated that Daniel and Mark would be startled when I exposed the "voyeuristic" nature of my presence on the Tortoise. Although, I was caught off-guard by their unruffled acknowledgment of my project, it was clear that Daniel and Mark's "unusual" response had much to do with the presence of the camera crew. The passengers on this trip had been prepared in advance to be observed by the documentary team. As such, even though I was not working with the camera crew, I simply numbered as one more of the already many "voyeurs" on this journey. In addition, the documentary teams' use of cameras made their observational activities comparatively more noticeable and intrusive than mine. Thus, my more low-key observational techniques constituted less of a threat to the passengers.

Still, while my observational techniques were somewhat different than those of the documentary team, I had to admit that my observational techniques were not necessarily any "better." Despite the fact that I routinely informed other passengers that I was engaged in a field research project, because my observation techniques were less overt than those of the camera crew, the people that I observed were often less aware of my "scientific gaze" (Denzin, 1995). While "modernist" researchers might consider this to be a strength of my observational strategy, this form of "uncontaminated" observation tends to obscure, rather than eliminate, the influences of the observer upon the observed (Denzin, 1994b; Harman, 1996; Schwandt, 1994). Thus, the documentary team's form of observation was a bit more "honest" than mine because the gaze of cameras alerted their subjects without ambiguity to the fact that they were being observed. Consequently, by utilizing overt observational techniques the camera crew created more "honest" opportunities for the passengers to exercise some control over the way that their "selves" were documented. However, simply because the overt use of cameras may be a somewhat more "honest" documentary technique, this does not imply that such techniques necessarily capture the "real" or "true" essence of their subjects. The presentation of the passengers' selves was indeed problematized by the cameras. The "collaboration" in self presentation (Goffman, 1959) that was facilitated by the cameras could also generate "simulated" (Baudrillard, 1988, 1994) departures from subjects' "normal" self presentations.

Reactivity and Negotiating the Representation of Self

After breakfast Jeff announced that he had a full slate of activities planned for the rest of the day. We were going to drive directly across the state to Indiana Dunes State Park. There we would have a swim in Lake Michigan an then make supper next to the beach. As we drove across Indiana in the muggy, mid-day heat, Jerry, one of the youngest male passengers, got out a pair of drum sticks and started clattering them on a variety of surfaces (e.g., the inner wall of the bus, wood paneling, plastic water bottles, etc.) to produce an interesting combination of sounds. He quickly drew the attention of a circle of nearby passengers as well as that of James, one of the film crew members.

Video Clip #2: www.socresonline.org.uk/3/1/video/vid2qt.html

It occurred to me as I observed this scene that the point of making a documentary on the Green Tortoise—or conducting a field research project, for that matter—was because it was an unusual or "weird," and therefore intriguing, setting. Thus, the interest that the documentary had for its potential viewers lay in capturing that "weirdness" on film; for the crew to make a film that would be interesting to people who were curious about the "weird" travel experience that the Green Tortoise offers, the film crew would have to make an effort to capture all of the unusual activities that developed during the course of our trip. However, the instantaneous and conspicuous attention of a camera had an effect that modified events. In a sense, because of the "simultaneity" of the recording procedure, the cameras could not help but convert the events they were filming into "performances." By gazing upon the activities of particular individuals, the cameras had a tendency to create a "center of attention." As the camera gazed at Jerry, his drumming became the focus of interest for a widening circle of people who then related to Jerry's drumming much as an audience would to a performer (e.g., cheering, clapping, etc.). Thus, the cameras had the effect of creating "performer-audience" relationships between the subjects of their gaze and those people who directed their gaze towards the "center" that had been created by the camera.

As the "performance-making" power of the cameras had a propensity to restructure the activities upon which they gazed, this process also had the result of heightening the interest and enthusiasm that the passengers had for those activities. That is, the gaze of the cameras had a doubly stimulating effect upon the passengers: the gaze of cameras not only created performances—and, thus, sources of entertainment—but they also conferred significance upon those performances (i.e., the gaze of the cameras implied that activities were "important enough" to warrant documentation). Visual media have a great deal of "power" in that this technology has the capacity to confer significance on people, objects and events merely by gazing upon them. That is, mundane objects and events can achieve an elevation in their perceived significance simply by becoming "objects of attention." This phenomenon is similar in nature to Baudrillard's (1996) distinction between seduction and meaning, "...I believe that, by also describing the sites of fascination, where meaning is supposed to implode with great flourish, you bestow beauty on that void and give meaning to what shouldn't have any" (1996, p. 35). More than merely contributing to the structure of identity in the postmodern social experience, visual media technology also define the boundary between the "real" world of the ordinary and the simulated sphere of the "extraordinary." Baudrillard (1988) argues that in the contemporary world of visual media imagery, the relationship between simulations and the phenomena that have been simulated becomes resynthesized:

> The cinema has absorbed everything—Indians, *mesas*, canyons, skies. And yet it is the most striking spectacle in the world. Should we prefer "authentic" deserts and deep oases? For us moderns, and ultramoderns, as for Baudelaire, who knew that the secret of true modernity was to be found in artifice, the only natural spectacle that is really gripping is the one which offers both the most moving profundity *and at the same time the total simulacrum of that profundity* (Baudrillard, 1988, p. 69-70, Emphasis in original).

Thus, in a postmodern, visual age, what is "real" is accessible with the greatest profundity through images. "Video, everywhere, serves only this end: it is a screen of ecstatic refraction" (Baudrillard, 1988, p. 37). Consequently, in producing "simulated" images of individuals, objects and events, visual media technology transform the status of these phenomena with respect to the sphere of "meaningful" cultural constructs. Via their simulations, the individuals, objects and events that have been simulated are inducted into the world wherein media products are "preserved": "Everything can have a second birth, the eternal birth of the simulacrum…which is, as we know, a repeat performance of the first, but its repetition *as something more real*" (Baudrillard, 1988, p. 41, Emphasis in original). Whereas unsimulated events wallow in eternal obscurity, in becoming simulated recorded images become "larger than life." Simulations exist in a state of preservation wherein they may be distributed to, and consumed by, potentially unlimited numbers of people who, in turn, may each exalt in the profound significance of the otherwise mundane phenomena that have been aggrandized in their simulation. Consequently, not only did the cameras generate a source of entertainment for the passengers, but the cameras elevated the degree to which the passengers tended to be stimulated by the profusion of simulacra that were created by the cameras gaze. The gaze of the cameras made a "spectacle" of the unusual events that drew the attention of the cameras and, therefore, stimulated passengers to indulge and glory in the "weirdness" that was associated with our Tortoise adventure.

Indeed, it was impossible to avoid sensing the palpable energy that emanated from Jerry's drumming performance. However, even as real and potent as the enthusiasm that surrounded the drumming performance happened to be, I could not avoid being disgruntled by the fact that Jerry's performance was a "simulation." Much as the performance may have been a spontaneous product of the unique environment that inhered within our well-documented Tortoise adventure, nevertheless, it had not been "real." In other words, the drumming "spectacle" had been driven and structured by the presence of the cameras. Without the gaze of the cameras the centrality of focus, the structure of the performance and, thus, the "significance" and the intensity of energy surrounding the event would not have existed. Although I had seen an abundance of weird and wacky events on the other Green Tortoise trips, at no time had any of those events taken on the structure of the drumming performance—nor had they exhibited such a self-indulgent celebration of "weirdness." As such, due to its departure from "reality," I felt more repulsed by Jerry's performance than drawn to it. Still, "simulated" as the drumming spectacle had been, it had been a very "real" and compelling event for many of the passengers on our bus; whether I liked it or not, the simulating presence of the cameras made such performances an integral and "real" component of the "simulated" journey in which we were taking part.

Beginning the Formal Interviews

While the cameras offered a unique source of entertainment for the passengers, challenges did remain for passengers as they struggled to manage their self-presentations under watchful gaze the cameras. After having supper in Indiana we woke the next morning in Wisconsin to find Jeff searching for a breakfast site along the banks of the Mississippi River. Following breakfast and a swim in the river, we loaded onto the bus and settled in for another long day of driving. Over the next twenty-four hours Jeff was hoping to traverse across much of the Midwest in order to arrive at Badlands National Park, on the west side of South Dakota, in time for a pre-dawn hike. Thus, this long day of driving provided the film crew with an opportunity to conduct brief interviews with each of the people on the bus.

This process created a stir throughout the bus because of the novelty that being interviewed offered for many of the passengers. The camera crew conducted their interviews by having Ken train his camera on one interviewee after another, while Amy handled a boom microphone and Debra kept an eye on the audio recording levels. The brief interviews were comprised of questions about the interviewees' names, occupations and their reasons for being on the Tortoise. Slowly, Ken worked his way over to Greg, a friendly German man, who was sitting next to me. Greg got a bit flustered under the glare of the camera. Greg explained, while the crew took a break after his interview, that he had not been able to understand Ken's questions clearly and, thus, he had been forced to fumble for answers. I tried to reassure Greg that he had done a good job in his interview. I also gave him some offhand advice about responding in German whenever he could not understand an interviewer's English. Greg laughed a bit uncertainly at my advice, and I soon understood why. In the midst of my chat with Greg I found that Ken was training his camera on me.

It is a very strange feeling to be on camera. There are various ways of dealing with the stress-related energy one may encounter while being "gazed" upon. Whenever Flaherty (1976) began filming "Nanook," he became overcome with laughter (Massot and Regnier, 1994). Also, in several instances, Inuit children who were being filmed by Massot and Regnier (1994) ran for hiding places when they came under the gaze of cameras. No matter how one compensates for the nervous energy that being on camera can produce (e.g., laughing, running away, acting like a nervous wreck, or creating a "performance"), in each case the camera affects one's behavior.

The process of being interviewed added a radical twist to my voyeuristic project. Whereas, in gazing upon the interactions between the film crew and passengers, I had been fascinated by the effects that I had perceived the film crew to be having upon the other passengers, in being interviewed my outward gaze suddenly was reflected backwards. That is, beyond feeling as though my voyeuristic activities had become "exposed" (Denzin, 1995, p. 49), my scientific gaze was suddenly reversed and synthesized with the gaze of the camera into an intense gaze of "double scrutiny." In being doubly scrutinized (i.e., gazing upon myself self-consciously and scientifically as an "object" filmmakers' gaze), I became preoccupied excessively with my presentation of self. Having been identified as "the resident sociologist" (quotation from the narration in *Songs of the Open Road*), I felt as though I needed to maintain "face" (Goffman, 1967) on a number of different levels. As a "professional sociologist" I felt responsible for creating the impression that I could analyze the challenges of identity construction in an age of "simulations" (Baudrillard, 1988; Denzin, 1995) without simultaneously suffering from those difficulties even while my own self image was undergoing simulation. In addition, I also felt responsible for offering samples of the kind of penetrating sociological insights that "could only come from someone with an advanced academic degree." And I wanted to do all of this while I avoided creating the impression that, due to my awareness of the various responsibilities under which I needed to bear up, my performance was not actually "a performance." Consequently, in this brief interview, I had a powerful introduction to the difficulties involved in sustaining a carefully crafted presentation of self before the unblinking stare of the camera.

In my on-camera interview, I became better able to empathize with the subjects of the voyeur's gaze. I learned that under the searching gaze of voyeurs engaging in even the most routine activities becomes a struggle. In addition, in being gazed upon by other voyeurs, I obtained a sense for the distortion of reality that can precipitate from encounters with voyeurs. While this may have been news to me, the documentary team understood all too well what corrupting effects their cameras' gaze might have upon the "truths" they wished to capture. Consequently, as part of the process of capturing the "real" experiences of Green Tortoise passengers, the documentary team also adopted measures to restructure their "documentary gaze" and, thereby, assisted passengers in the deconstruction of their "documentary selves."

Restructuring the Voyeur's Gaze

After our long day of driving across Minnesota, we stopped in a small city park to make dinner. Throughout the course of our meal teenagers from the town cruised through the park and gaped at our bus. While we ate dinner, Jeff gave us a preview of the next major stop on our trip, Badlands National Park. One reason that Jeff was excited about getting to the Badlands was that we would be having our first overnight camp out in the Park. Therefore, Jeff could look forward to enjoying a rare night of uninterrupted sleep. Another noteworthy element of our stop in the Badlands was that we were going to rendezvous with another Tortoise bus.

The Green Tortoise often operates two cross-country buses concurrently: one eastbound and the other westbound. Thus, sometimes the two buses are able to coordinate meetings in the middle of the country. Rendezvousing with the other bus sounded like it could make for an entertaining evening. Jeff explained that it was not unusual for big parties to result from encounters with other Tortoise buses. Furthermore, I thought that it would be interesting to compare the progress of our trip with another group of travelers who had not been exposed to the gaze of a documentary team's cameras.

It was well after dawn when we arrived at Badlands National Park—Jeff seemed to have a knack for making "gross miscalculations of time and distance" (Quote from an interview with a male passenger, named Dennis). We began our day by hiking along the Castle Rock trailhead that traced a line between the grassy plains of the Dakotas and the eroded contours of the Badlands. After our hike we took a tour of the park—including stops at the visitor center and the "company" town of Scenic. From Scenic we drove to a remote spot where we could go swimming.

When he had parked the bus, Jeff explained that we had arrived at the first place where it would be okay to swim nude and do "mud yoga." Jeff also explained that the camera crew was going to be hanging around. Thus, he thought it would be natural for some people to feel uncomfortable about skinny-dipping and, therefore, he insisted that anyone who felt the least bit uncomfortable about swimming in the nude should not be pressured to do so. "If you don't want to be caught in the nude, then wear a suit. If you don't care, you don't care." However, Jeff also added, "I, personally, am looking forward being nude and on film" (Dialogue transcription from *Songs of the Open Road*).

Video Clip #3: www.socresonline.org.uk/3/1/video/vid3qt.html

Good to his word, Jeff was one of the first people to have his clothes off and to plunge into the mud on the bank of a nearby stream. Despite the presence of the cameras, quite a few of the passengers cast aside their clothing and inhibitions, and joined Jeff in the mud. However, I was particularly surprised to observe that some of the most enthusiastic mud-bathers were the members of the documentary team. Amy shot footage of people rolling around in the mud for a while, but then she turned the camera over to Loni, a female passenger from the Netherlands. Loni then reversed her relationship to the gaze of camera by filming the documentary team, who had suddenly become the subjects of their own documentary.

The simple act of transferring their equipment into the hands of passengers modified the structure of the documentary team's voyeuristic project profoundly. By ceding control over the camera equipment, the film crew enabled the passengers to participate more fully in the construction of the documentary. With the cameras in the hands of the passengers, the subjects of the documentary were able to shoot footage that contributed to the construction of the tale of their own experiences (Issari and Paul, 1979; Mamber, 1974; Stoller, 1992). Furthermore, the camera crew's enthusiastic participation made it possible for their project to become more deeply embedded in the events that they were filming. As the film crew themselves became active participants in the "weirdness" of the Tortoise adventure, the documentation of events fell increasingly under the influence of "real" participants on the trip (i.e., passengers who had taken an interest in shooting footage and the camera crew who had become absorbed into the Tortoise's "unusual" experience). Nevertheless, the presence of the documentary team and their equipment could not help but continue to add an unusual "spin" to the structure of the trip. The principal source of this influence was rooted in the cameras' proclivity to generate their own source of excitement. Captivating as the attention of the cameras may have been for some, not everyone shared an equal passion for the excitement, "significance" or "reality" of events as they unfolded on our adventure trip.

An Instructive Encounter

When it became too cool and breezy to swim in the mud any longer, we sat on the dusty grass around the bus and bathed in the sun. Jeff wanted to proceed to the restaurant where he had arranged to meet the other bus, but he was voted down by all of the people who wanted to drink beer and listen to music. Happy hour carried on until Jeff spotted the other Tortoise bus.

As familiar as our own bus had become, it was still odd to see another big, green bus rolling along the hillside on the opposite side of the river. Rather than dawdling by the river any longer, Jeff got everyone loaded onto the bus and we set off for our rendezvous.

We were going to meet the eastbound bus at a nearby restaurant that was run by Native Americans. Shortly after we arrived at the restaurant the other bus appeared. The documentary team set to work immediately filming and collecting release forms from their new subjects. The restaurant was little more than a hut with a small counter and a few tables. Three women, who were behind the counter, were serving "Indian Tacos": fried bread with beans, salad, free-range beef and a selection of hot sauces. We remained at the restaurant while Jeff went on reconnaissance with the restaurant's owner to search for a suitable campsite. As night was beginning to fall, Jeff returned with the news that he had found a great campsite. We loaded into our respective buses and then drove a few miles from the restaurant to a dirt trail. Jeff turned onto the trail and then crept into the midst of an open field. Following a bit of indecisiveness, Jeff parked next to a sunken pit that was about forty feet across and ten feet deep. The pit served admirably as a meeting place and a fire circle.

Soon after a crackling bonfire had been set ablaze in the center of the pit, a loud call was raised for Jerry to play the drums. As Jerry began playing drums it became evident that the activities of the passengers on our bus were being influenced by the film crew's overt recording technique. The bonfire had transformed the pit into a blazing orange arena. The drummers, the firelight and the boisterous members of our bus created the kind of fantastic spectacle that made for great documentary footage. As the camera crew gazed attentively upon the drummers, the activities in the fire pit took on the structure of a staged performance. Jerry and several other people, who had joined him in the drumming, had become the centers of attention; they were "the performers," and as such they were distinguishable from the other people in the pit due to their being the focal points of attention—both of the documentary team as well as of the audience of passengers who cheered and responded with encouragement to their efforts.

Video Clip #4: www.socresonline.org.uk/3/1/video/vid4qt.html

The avid attention of the documentary team added to the excitement of this particular spectacle. That is, because the camera crew was so attentive to the performance in the fire pit, the "significance" of the event became elevated correspondingly. As the drummers and their audience began to feel that they were indeed involved in a "spectacular" event, their enthusiasm increased and so did the value of the spectacle for the documentary team. Indeed, these dynamics combined to generate a truly spontaneous and spectacular event. However, not everyone who was present was equally impressed by the fireside performance.

We did not hit it off very well with the people from the other bus. As the performance in the pit advanced, the people from the other bus slowly disappeared. As the people from our bus became more involved in the performance by the fire, the people from the other bus lost interest. Daniel told me that a few people from the other bus went so far as to suggest that the passengers on our bus were "a bunch of posers...You know, [like] we're just putting this on as an act" (Interview transcription). It was easy to understand how the performance in the fire pit could appear to be a "simulation"—because it certainly was. The fireside drumming performance was a consequence of the evolving integration of the documentary simulation into our Tortoise trip. However, the people from the eastbound Tortoise witnessed the fireside performance merely as the "artificial" conduct of blowhards doing their best to get their faces on camera. Because the people on the other Tortoise bus had not been exposed extensively to the cameras they did not share the same motivation or appreciation for "celebrations of weirdness" as did the passengers on our bus.

Later in the evening, while the drumming in the pit was still going strong, Susan and I stumbled across a small group of people who were almost undetectable outside the noise and the bright firelight in the pit. They were people from the eastbound bus who were trying to enjoy the fire, but who were also trying to avoid the drumming spectacle. I was struck by the contrast between the activities of the people inside versus those outside the fire pit: the people from the other bus were sitting a short distance from the rim of the pit, talking quietly, sipping beer and paying vague attention to someone in their midst who was strumming a guitar. Since their activities were not influenced by the focus of cameras, they were not stimulated to create a spectacle or to structure their entertainment. I could not help feeling a little envious of their calmer, more dignified composure. Early the next morning the eastbound Tortoise bus packed up and left without ceremony. Our meeting provided ample evidence that we were indeed proceeding in much different directions.

Transforming the Adventure

As we drove away from Badlands National Park during the next afternoon, Beth borrowed the camera crew's walkie-talkie and sent goofy messages to James who was driving the van. The camera crew had become very permissive of the passengers who wished to use their equipment. In fact, Daniel had begun working so closely with the documentary team that he achieved the honorary status of "sixth member of the camera crew." On one occasion Daniel drove the camera crew's van through the night because Chuck had become so starved for sleep that he had begun hallucinating as he was driving.

Over the next couple of days we drove through many of the scenic wonders and National Parks of Wyoming, Colorado and Utah.

Video Clip #5: www.socresonline.org.uk/3/1/video/vid5qt.html

Jeff arranged for our second camp out of the trip to be in Moab, Utah. Our day in Moab began with a raft trip on the Green River. After the raft trip, we returned to Moab, got some supplies and then drove to a riverside campsite that was set amidst giant slabs of red rocks. During dinner that evening Debra announced that she wanted to share a case of champagne she had purchased as a way of thanking everyone for being so cooperative with her documentary. The champagne celebration was, in fact, only the beginning of the entertainment for the evening. As we sipped champagne a number of people began beating on plastic buckets that they had taken into a large culvert running beneath a set of nearby train tracks. The tunnel added extra reverberation to the drumbeats and provided an environment in which the most spectacular group event of the trip could take place.

Spectacular group events are common to Tortoise trips and this one was similar in many ways to others that I have witnessed (McGettigan, 1997, unpublished). That is, the unconventional atmosphere on the Tortoise (e.g., tight living quarters, a lack of privacy, communal sleeping and eating arrangements, etc.) can cause its passengers to cling firmly to their conventional inhibitions. Generally, the tension between the passengers and the unconventional environment on the Tortoise builds until group events evolve that serve to "explode"—or "deconstruct" (Denzin, 1989b, 1994a)—the influences of conventional social constraints over the structure of the passengers' thoughts and behaviors. These are usually very energetic events due to the fact that they are fueled by the sudden release of tension that has been building-up for days or even weeks. As a result of these "deconstructive," tension-relieving events, passengers often feel more comfortable about flouting conventional social constraints for the balance of their journeys. On this trip, due to the influences of the documentary team, such tension-relieving events tended to be organized around visual spectacles. This night's performance was an even more fantastic visual spectacle than the drumming performance in the Badlands.

Video Clip #6: www.socresonline.org.uk/3/1/video/vid6qt.html

The dancers added to the booming resonance of the drumming by waving their flashlights as they wriggled in their makeshift discotheque. The people in the culvert danced and drummed for a couple of hours until they emerged as a worn out, sweaty mass, and then took a skinny-dip in the nearby river.

As much as such visual spectacles may have been perceived by "critics" (e.g., the passengers on the eastbound bus and myself) to have been an "artificial" contrivance, in a discussion related to this topic, Daniel suggested that the presence of the cameras had enabled he and others to "reflect" upon their identities in ways that would not have been possible otherwise. While, his initial reaction to the cameras had been to create an "epic" representation of himself, this impulse had faded as he developed a more insightful analysis of his "real self":

> ...I will admit that at first I thought, "Wow, you know, I really would like them to get pictures of me, you know, climbing a mountain." You know, the "epic," forever me. Immortal on film. But then I realized, you know, that's basically the uh...video version of making a face at a camera (Interview transcription).

As a result, while the documentary team captured images of passengers whose level of enthusiasm about participating in this Tortoise adventure had been intensified—much as Debra had predicted—the "indexicality" (Nichols, 1991) of the documentary simulation was not utterly compromised as a result. While long term exposure to the gaze of cameras had a tendency to stimulate and structure "performances," at the same time, being gazed upon for an extended period time also enabled some passengers to progress towards a deeper understanding, and more "verisimilar" (Lincoln and Denzin, 1994) presentation, of their identities.

The Self-Perpetuating Significance of the Simulacrum

During the next day we traveled from Bryce Canyon to Zion National Park. After a very late dinner in Zion we settled in for the last stage of the trip. Jeff was planning to drive throughout the night so that we could spend the final evening of our journey on the California coast. In the middle of the night—from 2:00 to 3:00 AM—we made a brief, nightmarish stop in Las Vegas. The lights of Las Vegas exploded out of the desert in such a shimmering conflagration that, combined with the stifling desert heat, it was not hard to imagine that we had arrived in Hell.

Video Clip #7: http://www.socresonline.org.uk/3/1/video/vid7qt.html

When dawn broke we had almost emerged from the Nevada desert. Upon arriving in California Jeff piloted the bus towards Bakersfield in order to drop off Andie, the first passenger to depart from our adventure trip. Andie had made arrangements to meet a friend at the Greyhound station in Bakersfield. Because our arrival in Bakersfield coincided roughly with the lunch hour, Jeff announced that we should make use of this stop to find refreshments. Most of the bus's compliment ate their noon meal at a deli that stood a stone's throw from the Greyhound station. After devouring a quick sandwich in the frigid deli, Susan and I returned to the fiery air of the afternoon and then joined the crowd on the shady sidewalk next to the bus. While we were waiting to get back on the road, a reporter from a local TV news station arrived with the intention of shooting footage of the Green Tortoise for the evening news. The presence of the reporter activated the documentary team, who, in a flash, had their cameras rolling as well.

Video Clip #8: http://www.socresonline.org.uk/3/1/video/vid8qt.html

The ensuing scene characterized many of the unique aspects of the motion picture documentation medium, while it also offered a demonstration of the manner in which the "significant" components of postmodern reality have become caught up in endless cycles of visual simulation (Baudrillard, 1988; Denzin, 1995). As much as motion picture cameras can be the *seekers* of spectacle, they can also be the *sources* of it. That is, the TV news reporter was interested in documenting a story about the Green Tortoise, but he became even more interested in the Tortoise when he discovered the presence of the documentary team. Thus, an important element of the reporter's "story" was that there was a film crew at work on the Tortoise. As a result, we were treated to a somewhat surreal spectacle of documentation: the local TV reporter had come to film the people on the Tortoise, but then he had found another film crew filming us; thus, he filmed the crew that was in the process of filming us, and he did this while the film crew that was filming us, filmed him as he filmed them. And to complicate matters further, as the camera crews filmed each other, the Tortoise passengers—whose experience the camera operators were intent upon documenting—gazed upon the spectacle created by the camera operators' simulation of each other, and wondered. In the end, it was difficult to decide where the simulation of our Tortoise adventure began and ended—or, as Baudrillard (1988. 19940 points out, if in fact reality was in any final way distinguishable from its simulation.

37

After this orgy of documentation we got on the bus and headed for the coast. We spent much of the day making a long, hot drive across California. Although Jeff had hoped to travel as far as Big Sur, we made it no further north than San Simeon State Park—still a strikingly beautiful beachfront location.

Video Clip #9: http://www.socresonline.org.uk/3/1/video/vid9qt.html

While we cooked and ate dinner, anticipation grew for the last drumming party that was being organized on the beach. The sparsely populated coast offered an ideal location to build another roaring bonfire. As Jerry and a woman, named Mannie, drummed on plastic buckets, a few passersby accompanied them on driftwood logs. The passersby remained in the shadows outside the firelight and, when they were encouraged to join in the "performance," they shrugged off the opportunity. It remained the case that kindred spirits still chose to remain outside the glow of the firelight and well beyond the gaze of the cameras. Ours had been a unique adventure that, while following a course that was similar to that of other Tortoise trips, had blurred the boundary between simulation and reality in the postmodern world.

Conclusion

The conception of self in contemporary culture has come to be influenced increasingly by, and defined through—but is not yet well-examined in relation to—various forms of visual media and simulations: "[Americans] are themselves simulation in its most developed state, but they have no language in which to describe it, since they themselves are the model" (Baudrillard, 1988, p. 28-29). Despite being influenced extensively by the world of visual simulations, it remains for most people an unusual, exciting—and, indeed, anxiety-provoking—experience to be gazed upon by motion picture cameras. Yet, it was through the novelty of being exposed to the motion picture documentation process that Green Tortoise passengers were able to deconstruct (Denzin, 1989b, 1994a) the "power" that visual media exercises over their definition of self. In other words, the gaze of the cameras made it possible for myself and the other subjects of the documentary "to visualize not only theory and culture as products of a complex visual cinematic apparatus, but to show how that apparatus entangles itself within the very tellings we tell" (Denzin, 1995, p. 200).

Therefore, in generating a "simulated" experience for the passengers on the Tortoise, the documentary team collaborated in the production of the transformative cultural critique that is the "real" substance of the Green Tortoise travel experience—and which, as it turns out, also happens to be the crucial subject matter that it was the goal of the documentary team to capture. In the end, the documentary team captured the "journey" into the identities of the passengers that they set out to record. In exposing themselves to the gaze of their cameras, the documentary team emphasized the fact that "truth" is not to be found merely in gazing upon others. Although it may not be possible to gaze upon truth no matter where one's camera is focused, it is through the unblinking eye of the camera that "a new form of self-awareness is produced, an understanding that moves to the core of the other's self" (Denzin, 1995, p. 218). Thus, the filming techniques of the camera crew emphasized that the virtue of gazing upon others—either in visceral or simulated form—is not to locate truth, but, rather to employ a "reflexive mechanism" through which we can come to be more aware of the contemporary "cinematic" influences that structure our own voyeuristic gazes.

References

Baudrillard, Jean, 1988. *America*. (Translated by Chris Turner.) Verso: New York.

Baudrillard, Jean, 1994. *Simulacra and Simulation*. Ann Arbor: University of Michigan Press.

Baudrillard, Jean, 1996. *Cool Memories II: 1987-1990*. (Translated by Chris Turner.) Durham: Duke University Press.

Becker, Howard, 1986. *Doing Things Together: Selected Papers*. Evanston: Northwestern University Press.

Denzin, Norman K., 1989a. *The Research Act: A Theoretical Introduction to Sociological Research Methods. Third Edition*. Englewood Cliffs: Prentice-Hall.

Denzin, Norman K., 1989b. *Interpretive Interactionism*. Newbury Park: Sage.

Denzin, Norman K., 1994a. "Postmodernism and Deconstructionism." Pp. 182-202 in *Postmodernism and Social Inquiry*. David R. Dickens and Andrea Fontana (Eds.). New York: The Guilford Press.

Denzin, Norman K., 1994b. "The Art and Politics of Interpretation." Pp. 500-515 in *Handbook of Qualitative Research*. Norman K. Denzin and Yvonna S. Lincoln (Eds.). Thousand Oaks: Sage.

Denzin, Norman K., 1995. *The Cinematic Society: The Voyeur's Gaze*. London: Sage.

Flaherty, Robert Joseph, 1976. *Nanook of the North*. (International Film Seminars) Home Vision.

Goffman, Erving, 1959. The *Presentation of Self in Everyday Life*. Garden City, N.Y.: Doubleday.

Goffman, Erving, 1967. *Interaction Ritual: Essays in Face to Face Behavior*. Garden City, N.Y.: Anchor Books.

Harman, Willis W. 1996. "The Shortcomings of Western Science." *Qualitative Inquiry* (2) 1: 30-38.

Issari, M. Ali, and Doris A. Paul, 1979. *What is Cinema Verite?* London: The Scarecrow Press, Inc.

Lincoln, Yvonna S., and Norman K. Denzin, 1994. "The Fifth Moment." Pp. 575-586 in *Handbook of Qualitative Research.* Norman K. Denzin and Yvonna S. Lincoln (Eds.). Thousand Oaks: Sage.

Mamber, Stephen, 1974. *Cinema Verite in America: Studies in Uncontrolled Documentary.* Cambridge: The MIT Press.

Massot, Claude, and Sebastien Regnier, 1994. *Nanook Revisited.* Princeton: Films for the Humanities.

McGettigan, Timothy, 1997. "Uncorrected Insight: Metaphor and Transcendence 'After Truth' in Qualitative Inquiry." *Qualitative Inquiry* 3 (3): 366-383.

McGettigan, Timothy, 1999. *Utopia on Wheels: Blundering Down the Road to Reality.* Lanham, MD: University Press of America

Nichols, Bill, 1991. *Representing Reality: Issues and Concepts in Documentary.* Bloomington: Indiana University Press.

Riesman, David, 1950. *The Lonely Crowd: A Study of the Changing American Character.* New Haven: Yale University Press.

Rothschild-Whitt, Joyce, 1979. "The Collectivist Organization: An Alternative to Rational-Bureaucratic Models." *American Sociological Review*, 44: (August) 509-527.

Schwandt, Thomas A. 1994. "Constructivist, Interpretivist Approaches to Human Inquiry." Pp. 118-137 in <u>Handbook</u> *of Qualitative Research.* Norman K. Denzin and Yvonna S. Lincoln (Eds.). Thousand Oaks: Sage.

Smith, Richard L., Clark McPhail, and Robert G. Pickens, 1975. "Reactivity to Systematic Observation with Film: A Field Experiment." *Sociometry*, (38) 4: 536-550.

Stoller, Paul, 1992. *The Cinematic Griot: The Ethnography of Jean Rouch.* Chicago: The University of Chicago Press.

CHAPTER THREE

Redefining Reality[1]

A Solution to the Paradox of Emancipation

Abstract

In this article I propose that a "redefined" standard of truth offers a means through which to develop a united theoretical and methodological framework for sociological science. I argue that, although human agency needs to be defined in terms that are antithetical to social structural constraint, agency and social structure must also be compatible and co-productive. As such, I also assert that the micro level of individual behavior is interactively linked to macro structures through the medium of three dimensional power. Finally, redefined truth facilitates a broader and more inclusive definition of sociological subject matter, while also advocating an improved alternative to the conventional notion of "good science."

Introduction

In what follows, I propose a solution to the paradox of emancipation by suggesting that actors have the capacity to "redefine reality" (McGettigan, 1998, 1999, 2000, 2001a). This solution has implications for a number of unresolved theoretical dilemmas. As evidenced in the three faces of power debate (Lukes, 1974, 2005), conventional approaches to sociological science employ methods that comply to a constrained definition of disciplinary subject matter. I argue that to observe the third face of power successfully one must expand one's definition of "good science" to more fully appreciate the multi-dimensional nature of empirical reality. In doing so, sociologists will be better able to conceptualize the linkages (Alexander, 1987; Ritzer, 2000b) between the various levels of social structure and the diverse fields of sociological inquiry.

Consideration of the role that power plays in the dynamics between actors and social structures varies according to one's definition of scientific truth and influences the way one conducts sociological science. As such, critics (Collins 1991, 1997; Denzin, 1997; Seidman 1991; Smith 1991, 1996) have accused conventional sociology of imposing exclusive constraints on knowledge while also endorsing endemically unjust features of the contemporary social environment. However, such critics have been unable to develop a comprehensive substitute for the flawed scientific epistemology that they disavow. In an effort to overcome the epistemological dilemmas of standpoint perspectives, I advance a redefined standard of truth that, I argue, permits social scientists to more adequately compass the terrain of sociological subject matter and also to fashion a coherent alternative to "good science."

---

[1]   This is an updated version of an article originally published in the *Electronic Journal of Sociology*: http://www.sociology.org/content/vol003.004/mcgettigan.html

Competing Views of Power

According to Lukes (1974, 2005) there are three dimensions of power. The one- dimensional view defines power as something that is expressed in observable relationships: verbal or physical struggles between antagonists. The two-dimensional view includes the influence of intention in power relationships. This perspective criticizes one-dimensional power theories for overlooking the degree to which power may invisibly impede observable power contests. The three-dimensional view of power suggests that power is even more insidious. Three-dimensional perspectives assert that actors' very own interests are shaped by power structures. Thus, actors are often secretly hoodwinked into doing the bidding of others, even while presuming to serve their own self-interests.

The pluralistic, or one-dimensional view of power maintains that power in a democratic system is distributed among competing groups. This perspective stresses that, although it is unequally distributed, everyone has some access to power. Thus, Dahl (1961) assumed that one needed only to observe the democratic representational process in action to witness the exercise of power.

Dahl's "intuitive idea of power" can be described as follows: "<u>A</u> has power over <u>B</u> to the extent that he can get <u>B</u> to do something that <u>B</u> would not otherwise do" (1957, p. 80). Power, in this sense, is operationalized as the ability of one actor to affect another, which Dahl and other pluralists believe may best be observed in decision-making situations. Overt conflict is a fundamental component of this operationalization of power. Dahl measured power in terms of an actor's ability to win decisions on key issues, which necessarily implies some disagreement, or in Lukes' words, "actual and observable, <u>conflict</u>" (1974, p.13).

Dahl's emphasis on studying "concrete, observable <u>behavior</u>" (Lukes 1974, p.12) had a dual purpose. First, Dahl's (1961) study was a reaction to elite studies of power (Mills 1956). Elite power theorists claim that instead of being distributed pluralistically, power is possessed by a limited number of power brokers. Thus, Dahl's study of the political environment of New Haven, Connecticut was intended to demonstrate that many groups, not just elites, won key decisions and therefore possessed power. Second, Dahl had a scientific motive: he wanted to practice "good science," which implies a break with conceptual, philosophical issues in favor of studying observable behavior that is subject to conventional scientific analysis.[1]

Early critics of Dahl, proponents of what Lukes calls the two-dimensional view of power (Bachrach and Baratz 1970), argued that pluralist restrictions on the operationalization of power, that were intended to serve a particular definition of "good science," discounted an important facet of power: the mobilization of bias. The mobilization of bias is a "bias in favour of the exploitation of some kinds of conflict and the suppression of others" (Lukes 1974, p.16). Bachrach and Baratz claim that those who are in power exercise control over organizational agendas by making "nondecisions." Nondecisions are conscious choices made by agenda-setters that result "in suppression or thwarting of a latent or manifest challenge to the values or interests of the decision-maker" (Bachrach and Baratz 1970, p. 44). Issues that conflict with the

---

[1] This tradition in social science is closely related to what is often referred to as positivism. Turner (1987) describes positivism as "the use of theory to interpret empirical events and, conversely, the reliance on observation to assess the plausibility of theory" (1987, pp. 156-157). Although positivism has been criticized, reviled and renamed--Isaac (1987) pronounced positivism dead at the hands of Popper (1959) and refers to its descendant as "empiricism"--it remains an influential, if not the dominant, paradigm in sociology.

interests of agenda-setters may, therefore, be easily suppressed simply by failing to allocate time for their consideration. For example, political parties often enhance the perception of unanimity by failing to yield podium time to radical splinter groups during national conventions. In this way, power may be exercised quite effectively without creating any visible conflict, which, in turn, creates a problem for the practice of "good science" according to Dahl's definition. That is, Bachrach and Baratz point out--in agreement with the notions of other important scholars (Chomsky, 1996; Domhoff, 2002; Foucault, 1977; Mills, 1956)--that there are a variety of relatively "invisible" social dynamics that extensively mold the contours of observable reality. Therefore, without engaging the quality of mind (Mills, 1959) necessary to conceptualize the domain of conventionally invisible social phenomena, one's observations of empirical reality will be flawed at best.

However, despite Bachrach and Baratz's strong criticism of the one-dimensional view of power, they in turn make the dubious assertion that nondecisions are still observable in the conventional sense (1970, p. 50). Bachrach and Baratz claim that nondecisions are observable if one considers "potential issues." Thus, nondecisions may remain invisible to the naked eye, but, according to Bachrach and Baratz, nondecisions can enter the range of the observable if one bears in mind the existence of invisible, subversive challenges to authority--which is what Mills, not Dahl, tends to argue.

Oddly, although they appear to have incorporated "unobservable" criteria into their operationalization of power, Bachrach and Baratz (1970, pp. 49-50) still insist, along with Dahl, that to avoid reducing the scientific analysis of power to a branch of "moral philosophy," observable conflict must be present for power relationships to exist. That is, they claim that if no observable conflict is discernible in social relationships, then there is no way to judge accurately whether "consensus is genuine or instead has been enforced through nondecision-making" (1970, p. 49). Thus, in the end, Bachrach and Baratz support the same constraints on sociological subject matter--and therefore they end up advocating much the same definition of "good science"--that they criticized Dahl for adopting.

Lukes suggests that the conflict to which Bachrach and Baratz refer "is between the interests of those engaged in nondecision-making and the interests of those they exclude from a hearing within the political system" (Lukes 1974, p. 20). While, according to Lukes, this is a broader view of interests than that which is subscribed to by many pluralists, it remains a restricted definition. That is, Lukes argues that Bachrach and Baratz's definition is limited to what may be identified as "subjective interests" or those interests that "are consciously articulated and observable" (1974, p. 20). But this, Lukes contends, still sustains too narrow a view of interests and too great a dependence on observable conflict if one is to effectively define the full scope of power and the range of its invisible effects on observable reality.

> The trouble seems to be that both Bachrach and Baratz and the pluralists suppose that because power, as they conceptualize it only shows up in cases of actual conflict, it follows that actual conflict is necessary to power. But this is to ignore the crucial point that the most effective and insidious use of power is to prevent such conflict from arising in the first place (Lukes 1974, p. 23).

Lukes (1974, pp. 24-25) proposes that power relationships may be comprised by latent conflict, or what he describes as "a contradiction between the interests of those exercising power and the real interests of those they exclude." Real interests are the goals and desires that actors "would want and prefer, were they able to make the choice" (Lukes 1974, p. 34). In many cases, Lukes suggests, actors are not able to make the choices they would prefer because their conscious, subjective interests have been insidiously manipulated by invisible exercises of power.

For example, the socio-cultural context of the early twenty-first century USA tends to inscribe its citizens with "tastes" (Bourdieu, 1984; McGettigan, 1999; Ritzer, 2002a) for private homes, automobiles, computers, credit cards, cell phones, and fast food. Generally, we do not view our appetite for such cultural products as the work of social coercion. However, if we were to be situated in a markedly different cultural context, let's say sixteenth century Hudson Bay Inuit culture, then our desires would run more in the direction of warm fur-lined clothing, well-constructed igloos, skin-covered kayaks, and raw seafood. In such a context, it would be preposterous to lust after Big Macs because the extant cultural system would exert neither the impetus to seek, nor would it include any of the essential means to produce such delicacies. Thus, the third face of power works as a remarkably effective, macro-level *social glue* because of the way that it "encourages" individuals to apply themselves insatiably to the pursuit of those things that extant cultural systems are designed to provide. Conveniently, these selfsame forces facilitate the reproduction of the cultural context within which individuals are embedded (Willis 1977, Burawoy, 1979): our hunger for automobiles effectively sustains the viability of numerous global industries that are bent on satisfying consumer desires, e.g., petroleum, steel, shipping, etc. Automobile-lust also propels infrastructure development for an expanding automobile culture (Schlosser, 2001).

Therefore, the third face of power can be perceived as a thoroughly enveloping blanket of power that "steers" micro-level individual behavior toward activities and goals that bring about the reproduction of prevailing cultural contexts. Whether such cultural coercion should be considered "good" or "evil" is a matter of some debate. Since the preponderance of our humanity (Mead, 1934; Wiley, 1994) is accessible only through extensive communion with manipulative cultural environments, one should, seemingly of necessity, concede that there are positive aspects of cultural domination. However, members of some countercultures (McGettigan, 1999; Wolfe, 1968) and proponents of popular theoretical perspectives have, with qualifications, advanced arguments to the contrary (Lemert, 1999; Marx, 1906; Seidman, 1991). Nonetheless, putting aside the question of good versus evil forms of social power, it must be understood that cultural contexts are imbued with a subtle, invisible third face of power that thoroughly envelopes, and largely determines, the thoughts, behaviors, and goals of individual social actors. [1]

---

[1] Foucault (1980) notes that an important defining moment in his understanding of power occurred when he realized its "positive" effects.

> What makes power hold good, what makes it accepted, is simply the fact that it doesn't only weigh on us as a force that says no, but that it traverses and produces things, it induces pleasure, forms knowledge, produces discourse. It needs to be considered as a productive network which runs through the whole social body, much more than as a negative instance whose function is repression (1980, p. 119).

Critics of Lukes (Parsons 1960; Arendt 1969; Mann 1986) have claimed that because of this "positive" dimension of power one may disregard Lukes' negatively characterized third-dimension of power. They suggest that Lukes'

Indeed, exercises of the third face of power often result in what appears to be consensus, but such quietude can, Lukes argues, in fact be evidence of the most coercive face of power (Gaventa, 1980). Thus, Lukes suggests that one cannot capably analyze power or observable social reality without taking into account the dimensions of power that serve to structure events prior to their enactment in empirical reality. Yet, despite the fact that Lukes argues that it is essential to acknowledge the existence and effects of all three dimensions of power (i.e., the individual, organizational, and cultural levels of power), he also maintains that there are inescapable dilemmas that prevent agreement upon the definition of power's third face.

Lukes (1974, p. 26) states that power is "one of those concepts that is ineradicably value-dependent." This means that every definition of power is based upon value-assumptions and, therefore, any particular definition may only be applied situationally--never universally. However, Lukes adds that even though every definition of power is limited, some definitions nonetheless "extend further and deeper than others" (Lukes 1974, p. 26).

Lukes argues that the concept of interests is akin to power in that it is also a value-dependent, "irreducibly evaluative notion" (1974, p. 34). Furthermore, he notes that:

> different conceptions of what interests are are associated with different moral and political positions. Extremely crudely, one might say that the liberal takes men as they are and applies want-regarding principles to him, relating their interests to what they actually want or prefer, to their policy preferences as manifested by their political participation. The reformist, seeing and deploring that not all men's wants are given equal weight by the political system, also relates their interests to what they want or prefer, but allows that this may be revealed in more indirect and sub-political ways--in the form of deflected, submerged or concealed wants or preferences. The radical, however, maintains that men's wants may themselves be a product of a system which works against their interests, and, in such cases, relates the latter to what they would want and prefer, were they able to make the choice (Lukes 1974, p. 34).

While the three-dimensional, or radical, view of power may be a deeper and more thorough-going analysis of power, Lukes admits it is still a value-dependent notion. The value-dependency of the three-dimensional view of power in turn leads to an acute and as yet unsolved problem: the paradox of emancipation.

The Paradox of Emancipation

For Lukes to identify an exercise of power, he must be able to address "the double claim that $\underline{A}$ acts (or fails to act) in a certain way and that $\underline{B}$ does what he would otherwise not do" (1974, p.

conception of power is entirely negative and, given that social power creates consensus and often generates socially constructive outcomes, these positive aspects of power imply that Lukes' conception is patently false. However, I maintain that the positive and negative functions of power may only be properly conceived in connection with a thorough understanding of the third dimension of power. Positive functions of power may or may not be "good" for social actors. I believe the positive functions of power must still be judged by a redefined standard of truth or else one's definition of "good" will still be too strongly affected by organizational and societal interests.

41). To clearly recognize an exercise of power, one must first identify a "relevant counterfactual." A relevant counterfactual is a referent through which one may detect the interruption of an actor's interests by the imposition of another set of interests. For example, supporters of one and two-dimensional views of power argue that observable conflict--actors visibly manipulating the behavior of others--suffices as an unambiguous relevant counterfactual. Thus, according to this definition, power relationships exist only when A observably gets B to do something B would not otherwise do, e.g., parents sending reluctant children to bed, or police assaulting protestors with water cannons. However, in the case of the three-dimensional view of power identifying a relevant counterfactual becomes more complicated. The definition of the third face of power implies that events in empirical reality, as well as observers' perceptions of those events, are distorted by social power. Lukes states:

> in general, evidence can be adduced (though by nature of the case, such evidence will never be conclusive) which supports the relevant counterfactuals implicit in identifying exercises of power of the three-dimensional type. One can take steps to find out what it is that people would have done otherwise (1974, p. 50).

Although Lukes cites several interesting examples, he never explains specifically how to identify a relevant counterfactual for the third face of power. Thus, Lukes takes the discussion of power to a point where he challenges the limitations that have been imposed upon its definition by other theorists. However, Lukes fails to follow through by offering a means with which his conception of power can be employed to produce a more competent evaluation of observable social events.

Lukes does not specify a method for identifying relevant counterfactuals because he claims power is such a value-dependent concept that it is impossible to develop a consistent power-identification process. Thus, he believes that there are ways to identify counterfactuals-- and, thereby, exercises of the third face of power--but they depend in each case upon the values of the observer. Another reason that Lukes never specifies a consistent means with which to identify relevant counterfactuals for the third face of power is because he never clearly defines a model of real interests. And Lukes probably never proposed a specific method for identifying real interests because doing so precipitates certain seemingly insoluble problems. Lukes discusses two alternatives implicit in the identification of real interests:

> (1) that A might exercise 'short-term power' over B (with an observable conflict of subjective interests), but that if and when B recognizes his real interests, the power relationship ends: it is self-annihilating; or (2) that all or most forms of attempted or successful control by A over B, when B objects or resists, constitute a violation of B's autonomy; that B has a real interest in his own autonomy; so that such an exercise of power cannot be in B's real interests (1974, p. 33).

Following this, Lukes states that the first alternative is a "licence for tyranny," while the second alternative "furnishes an anarchist defense against it" (1974, p. 33). Thus, implied within the very definition of real interests is a power struggle: to define interests for other actors is to impose one's own views about what is "right and wrong" upon the events that one

48

observes, whereas failing to define real interests means that one has chosen not to recognize the occurrence of such subtle exercises of power. Although, strictly speaking, these alternatives may not represent a dichotomy, they do appear to represent the only available options for identifying exercises of the third face of power: to impose one's own value system or to relativistically avoid making any kind of judgment about the invisible effects of power on the course of social events. Recognizing the problematic consequences of both alternatives, Lukes refuses to embrace either one.

Benton (1981) labeled the conceptual impasse at which Lukes arrives the "paradox of emancipation."

> In its simplest form this is the problem of how to reconcile a conception of socialist practice as a form of collective self-emancipation with a critique of the established order which holds that the consciousness of those from whom collective self-emancipation is to be expected is systematically manipulated, distorted and falsified by essential features of that order. If the autonomy of subordinate groups (classes) is to be respected then emancipation is out of the question; whereas if emancipation is to be brought about, it cannot be self-emancipation. I shall refer to this problem as the 'paradox of emancipation' (Benton 1981, p. 162).

Thus, Benton asserts that "emancipation" can neither be engineered in the minds of the subjugated masses, nor implemented through the machinations of tyrants: in both cases, coercive power undermines the goal of emancipation. However, Benton bases his dismissal of the potential for identifying real interests on misleading grounds, i.e., because actors cannot completely overcome the influences of ideological systems Benton concludes that it is not possible for individuals to define, or to act upon their real interests. This neglects an important point that Lukes was trying to make: just because ideological systems generally deny the possibility of actors' emancipation does not mean that actors lack real interests. In other words, even though actors may not be able to free themselves from their ideological straight-jackets, the third face power may still be operationalized and analyzed in terms of *a conceptual definition* of real interests. Still, even though Benton makes a number of invalid assumptions about real interests, Benton's paradox of emancipation does raise important issues that Lukes' view of power ultimately fails to resolve.

Benton (1981, p. 164-5) claims that Lukes evokes the paradox of emancipation by suggesting that power may be exercised over an actor "with an observable conflict of subjective interests" (1974, p. 33) while still preserving an actor's real interests. However, Lukes never suggests that power may be exercised over an actor in the actor's real interests. Lukes does propose that idea as an alternative, but one that he finds unacceptable. Lukes says that of the two given alternatives, tyranny vs. anarchy:

> I am inclined to adopt the first, the dangers of which may be obviated by insisting on the empirical basis for identifying real interests. *The identification of these is not up to A, but to B*, exercising choice under conditions of relative autonomy and, in particular, independently of *A*'s power (Lukes 1974, p. 33).

Although Lukes makes it clear that he leans toward the merits of value-based evaluations of power, it is a mistake to conclude that Lukes abandons his operationalization of power to the paradox of emancipation. If Lukes had explicitly adopted the tyrannical approach to defining real interests, then he would also have embraced the paradox of emancipation: he would have stated that the only way to define real interests would be to impose one's value-based assumptions on events in social reality. However, Lukes says that he is inclined to the tyrannical alternative, but then he stipulates qualifications to this option that seem to contradict it. Whereas the tyrannical alternative states "that $\underline{A}$ might exercise 'short-term power' over $\underline{B}$" (Lukes 1974, p. 33) in $\underline{B}$'s real interests, Lukes' qualified acceptance of that alternative--which sounds suspiciously like the second option--is that $\underline{B}$ must identify $\underline{B}$'s real interests independently of $\underline{A}$'s power. Although this appears to be a contradiction--or a way for Lukes to avoid making a choice--I think Lukes was straddling the two alternatives, tyranny vs. anarchy, in deference to an as-yet-to-be articulated alternative.

Lukes rejects the idea that real interests can be defined by reference to a particular model of interests for two reasons. First, he thinks power is such a value-bound concept that it is not subject to universal definitions. Second, because privileging a particular model would provide in his words, a license for tyranny. On the other hand, Lukes did not embrace the relativism that Bradshaw (1976) claims he did, because he expressly rejects the anarchy inherent in that alternative. Thus, one question that the paradox of emancipation raises is: how can real interests be defined in such a way that one can consistently identify exercises of the third face of power while not privileging a particular set of interests and while also avoiding a collapse into moral relativism? A second question the paradox of emancipation raises, that is more immediately relevant to the practice of "good science," is: how can observers within real social contexts consistently identify invisible exercises of power? I think Lukes offers a potential solution to this apparent paradox when he suggests that autonomy is a real interest.

Autonomy and Real Interests

The purpose of explicating the third face of power is to facilitate a more complete understanding of empirical reality: observable social environments cannot be fully understood without a grasp of the invisible and multi-dimensional social forces that construct the landscape of what and how we "see." However, the definition of radical power seems to imply that social actors, due to the omnipresence of invisible social power, are incapable of identifying exercises of radical power--or, in the language of another sociological debate (Bourdieu, 1984; Giddens, 1984; Ritzer, 2000b, pp. 521-552), social structures inescapably *determine* the entire scope of human thought and action. The deterministic argument maintains that social actors are nothing more than the unwitting pawns of social power structures. In other words, although actors may believe that invisible social power exists, because they are incapable of "seeing" precisely how they are affected by invisible societal influences, they are unable to struggle against or in any way act independently of such forms of power.

Nevertheless, one potential solution to the problem of identifying radical power is to conceptually construct its antithesis. Despite the fact that Lukes does not assert an explicit model of real interests, he does state that a social actor "has a real interest in his own autonomy" (1974, p. 33). Thus, Lukes' argument suggests that social actors' "real interests" are subverted through *external* impositions of power. In other words, according to Lukes' characterization of the third face of power, that which prevents actors from choosing to do what they "would otherwise do" is an imposition of radical power that breaches the autonomy of individual social actors. Therefore, following the logic of Lukes' argument, if an actor were "autonomous"--if the third face of power did not breach actors' individual sovereignty--then the influences that are responsible for the corruption of actor's real interests would not be effected. Purely for the sake of argument, we state that "autonomous actors",[1] due to their imagined freedom from the influences of coercive power, would not be disconnected from their real interests.

Certainly, a completely autonomous individual is something that does not and, for a wide variety of reasons, cannot exist in reality. However, that is precisely why this is such a useful concept for the purposes of the present discussion. Autonomy is that which cannot exist within an all-determining system of social control. If autonomy exists, then societal control cannot be absolute. That said, if one were able to identify certain conditions under which autonomy could exist within an environment of pervasive social determination--if, for example, one could identify a mechanism through which individuals could redefine the social landscape by creating "spaces" within which they could exercise autonomy--then one could also locate with specificity the phenomenon of agency. Thus, autonomy establishes a conceptual counterfactual for determining when the third face of power is being exercised and when it is not. As such, the concept of autonomy provides a means for resolving the paradox of emancipation.

Employing autonomy as a model of real interests arguably evades both snares, tyranny vs. anarchy, of the paradox of emancipation. First of all, rather than tyrannically defining a set of interests for actors, defining real interests in terms of autonomy asserts that it is up to individuals to decide what their real interests are. However, such a solution appears to plunge straight into the second snare of the paradox of emancipation: relativity. Nevertheless, if one could discover a way to find autonomy at work in real--as opposed to ideal, utopian, or purely conceptual--social environments, then one could argue that the definition of real interests may conceivably be governed by the ultimate standard: truth. [2]

---

[1] Once again, the goal here is simply to develop a concept for the purposes of illustrating a point. Under no circumstances should this statement be interpreted to mean that ideally autonomous actors either can or should walk the earth: they can't and they don't.

[2] Foucault (1972) argues that it does not make sense to disengage the concepts of knowledge and truth from power:

> The exercise of power perpetually creates knowledge and, conversely, knowledge constantly induces effects of power...Knowledge and power are integrated with one another, and there is no point in dreaming of a time when knowledge will cease to depend on power; this is just a way of reviving humanism in a utopian guise (1972, p.52).

> ...truth isn't outside power, or lacking in power: contrary to a myth whose history and functions would repay further study, truth isn't the reward of free spirits, the child of protracted solitude, nor the privilege of those who have succeeded in liberating themselves. Truth is a thing of this world: it is produced only by virtue of multiple forms of constraint. And it induces regular effects of power (1972, p. 131).

I agree that, in reality, there is a dynamic, productive relationship between knowledge and power. However, my point is simply to emphasize that knowledge and power are distinct concepts. And given that knowledge and power are distinct entities, even though power effectively distorts most knowledge in reality, it is still conceivable to imagine knowledge that is distinct from power. If, indeed, there is no knowledge that is independent of power, if truth is wholly the captive and product of power, then truth would have to be the result of the arbitrary determination

Kernohan (1989), however, argues that power and real interests should not be defined in terms of autonomy for a number of reasons. First, he suggests that it is circular reasoning to define power in terms of real interests and then to "characterize real interests in terms of their autonomy from the effects of power" (1989, p. 713). Secondly, he argues that one should not "identify power using a definition phrased in terms of intentions or wants, because intentions and wants may themselves be the creations of power" (1989, p. 716). And third, the term to be defined should not reoccur in its definition. In other words, "power must be defined prior to locating responsibility for its exercise" (1989, p. 722). Kernohan concludes by saying that:

> human agency is not the place to look for an adequate conception of power. If radical power exists, it will distort human agency by manipulating the beliefs and desires that ground rational decision making. A definition of social power in terms of human agency will be made difficult by the absence of a concept of a pure and unadulterated agent on which to base it. The existence of the power of one person over another is a social fact, not a material one; people do not have power because of an intrinsic property of themselves, but because of the social relations in which they are embedded (1989, p. 726).

This is a debatable conclusion, and one that somewhat contradicts a point Kernohan makes earlier when he observes that "[i]t is important to Lukes, as it should be to any social theorist, to give an account of power which comprehends power exercised through the manipulation of perceived interests" (1989, p. 714). Kernohan seems to be saying that even though it is important to account for human agency in theories of power, because a definition of autonomous agents "will be made difficult," the effort should be abandoned.

I agree that such a definition is essential and that it is difficult, but I reject the suggestion that the goal of defining agency in relationship to social power should be abandoned. Also, I do not think it is circular reasoning to operationalize exercises of the third face of power and real interests in terms of autonomy. There is an important difference between <u>defining power</u> and <u>identifying exercises of power</u>. Critics (Isaac 1987; Wartenberg 1990) of the "three faces of power" debate have argued that the "definition" of power that Dahl (1957) began with and that later theorists built upon was not a definition but, rather, an operationalization of power. Whereas, in fact, there are two definitions of power: "power to" and "power over." "Power to" may be defined as "a property, capacity, or the wherewithal to effect things" (Isaac 1987, p. 74): this is the type of power that makes it possible for people to move their arms, to dream, to get out of bed in the morning, and, generally speaking, to cope with, and live life as unique individuals. On the other hand, "power over" can be defined as having "possession of control or command over others" (Wartenberg 1990, p. 18). "Power over" refers to the sociological dimensions of power through which the minds and activities of individuals are governed, manipulated, cultivated, corrupted, and sometimes destroyed (Gramsci, 1992). Indeed, despite the fact that Kernohan claims that "people do not have power because of an intrinsic property

---

of power and it would be impossible for "intellectuals," despite what Foucault suggests, to detach "the power of truth from the forms of hegemony, social, economic and cultural, within which it operates..." (Foucault 1972, p.133). Thus, knowledge is not only conceptually distinguishable from power, but, as I will demonstrate, knowledge is also an important vehicle through which power is generated, exercised and, occasionally, undone.

of themselves" (1989, p. 726), it is essential to acknowledge that social power, i.e., "power over", cannot exist in a vacuum. People must exist, and they must be endowed with intrinsic capabilities to effect things, i.e., "power to", or else manifestations of social power become untenable.

Thus, the "three faces of power debate" is not so much a debate over the definition of power as it is a debate about the various ways that exercises of coercive power affect actors' interests. The difficulty that Lukes (1974) encountered was not how to define the third face of power, but how to establish a counterfactual that could be used to consistently identify exercises of the third face of power. Thus, it is not circular reasoning to correlate autonomy and power, to do so is simply to employ a counterfactual.

Therefore, I maintain that the idealized concept of autonomy offers a theoretical solution to the paradox of emancipation. However, thus far this solution has only addressed the first question that the existence of radical power raises (i.e., how can we define real interests without privileging a particular set of interests and while also avoiding a collapse into moral relativism?). Yet, the whole point of developing a conceptual means with which to identify radical power is to achieve a broader understanding of social reality: to explain how people who are embedded within manipulative social environments can overcome the constraints that limit their understanding of society.

Whereas the theoretical resolution of the paradox of emancipation requires that one employs an extra-empirical (i.e., "ideal autonomy") conceptual mechanism, the purpose of resolving the paradox of emancipation is not to suggest that the only way to confront radical power is to escape reality. Rather, the purpose of resolving the paradox of emancipation is to expand the definition of empirical reality such that the problematic nature of the relationship between societal coercion and individual autonomy can be situated within it. In other words, the only worthwhile solution to the paradox of emancipation is one that situates the ideal within the real.

From the Ideal to the Real

The definition of truth that precipitates from defining real interests in terms of autonomy has strong similarities to Habermas' "ideal speech situation." An ideal speech situation is a theoretical interaction based upon "pure intersubjectivity," wherein there is "complete symmetry in the distribution of assertion and dispute, revelation and concealment, prescription and conformity, among the partners of communication" (Habermas 1970, p. 371). Pure intersubjectivity implies that there should be no restrictions on, or distortions of, the meaning interactants wish to share. In an ideal speech situation, each communicant would be able to completely understand the meaning that others expressed because the distorting influences of power would be neutralized.

People have argued that Habermas is naïve for proposing that communication could ever be carried out under such ideal circumstances. Critics (Lukes 1982; Turner 1987, p. 160; Clegg 1989, p. 94) have suggested that Habermas' presumption that truth could only be achieved in a coercion-free environment is not just totally unrealistic, but it also avoids the crucial problem that must be addressed: how do people who are enveloped by coercion achieve a better understanding of the reality that distorts their consciousness? Thus, critics have maintained that if Habermas' solution to the problem of understanding radical power is only applicable in an imaginary, coercion-free universe, then his solution is not really of value in our coercion-permeated reality.

I agree that Habermas' definition of an ideal speech situation is far removed from the less-than-ideal reality of experience. Further, I agree that any solution to the theoretical problem of defining actors' ability to be emancipated from the cognition-manipulating intrusions of coercive power must be situated within our coercion-permeated reality.[1] That is, since it is the objective of social science to explain empirical social reality instead of utopian alternatives to that reality, the discussion of abstract and conceptual dimensions of power must inform our understanding of _real_ agents in _real_ social situations. While Habermas' ideal speech situation ultimately fails to make this reconnection with reality, there remain elements of his theory that provide important insights into the process through which actors can generate moments of ideally autonomous activity, i.e., agency, within the coercive confines of social reality.

Habermas recognizes that "pure intersubjectivity is an idealization" (1970, p. 372); it is not supposed to be a description of the reality that does or could exist. However, his point is that intersubjective communication is _oriented to_ the truth. Habermas asserts that even though all successful interactions are situated in coercive environments, communication must still be premised upon an effort to obtain truth or it will be meaningless.

Truth in Habermas' terms has specifically to do with communicants' ability to understand as fully as possible the meaning that other social actors wish to impart. A state of truth would be one in which all social actors could express themselves with perfect clarity while also comprehending the total content of messages from other interactants. Whereas such a perfect environment is impossible in reality, nevertheless, no matter how distorted an

---

[1] Such a definition must also be able to explain why agency, if it exists in the social reality that is permeated by structural coercion--as I argue that it must--causes that structural coercion to be _reproduced_ rather than being _undone_ as it is in Habermas' ideal speech situation. I disagree with Habermas' assertion that a utopian environment is the necessary result of agency--indeed, I have argued elsewhere that "redefinitions of reality" are much more likely to produce "mobile utopias" (McGettigan, 1999), or contexts that are embedded within, and are dependent upon, mainstream society, but that also facilitate fleeting localized counter-normative spaces.

Even Habermas argues that for ideal speech to develop it must be situated in an elaborate social context. For people to communicate intersubjectively, they must first master "linguistic competence, [and] basic qualifications of speech and symbolic interaction (role-behavior), which we may call communicative competence" (Habermas 1970, p 367). In other words, for people to find a way to free themselves from social coercion, they must first master and obey an extensive structure that defines meaning in communication. One might argue that, in saying this, Habermas contradicts himself: rather than making the case that communication can generate a reduction in societal constraint, Habermas is demonstrating that actors are never free from social power, i.e., even when it appears as though actors are creating an environment in which they are removing the constraints of coercive power from their interpersonal communication, instead what they are doing is demonstrating that structural constraint is the precondition, the medium, and the result of intersubjective communication. However, one might also argue that, just because agency exists--and even though it must be defined in terms that are oppositional to social coercion--does not necessarily imply that agency and social structure are incompatible. Whereas agency may only manifest in contexts that incorporate individual-level opposition to social power, the consequences of its exercise are not sufficient to completely unmake society. Society is simply too large and adaptable to be threatened by the activities of individual agents. Instead, the negation of hegemonic constraint that agency generates is more likely to be "absorbed" (e.g., the work of entrepreneurs, inventors, and scientists, while often revolutionary, in many ways leads to modifications to, rather than the dissolution of, the social environment in which it is carried out) by society and generally serves to extend and readapt, rather than dismantle, society.

environment may be, the act of communication--the act of establishing an intersubjective context of mutual understanding--can generate a microcosm of that ideal environment. Herein lies the crucial process through which the ideal (i.e., limited exercises of autonomy as expressions of individual agency) can be understood to operate within the real (i.e., social contexts that are pervaded by invisible mechanisms of social control and manipulation).

According to Habermas, before meaning can be shared between communicants, they must first establish an environment of mutual comprehension. Communicants accomplish this feat by demonstrating their "communicative competence":

> ...in order to participate in normal discourse the speaker must have at his disposal, in addition to his linguistic competence, basic qualifications of speech and symbolic interaction (role-behavior), which we may call communicative competence. This communicative competence means the mastery of an ideal speech situation (Habermas 1970, p. 367).

In the course of communicating, actors do not simply spew information at each other. Rather they must begin by establishing the grounds upon which meaning can be exchanged cooperatively. Social power distorts knowledge through communication two ways: 1. It structures subjective interests (i.e. it tells people what to think); and, 2. Because power tells people what to think they often ignore what others are trying to say. An intersubjective environment must be established even if it is one's intention to deceive because if communicants want their partners to understand what *they* have to say, then they must first try to grasp the subjective thoughts of their partners. Therefore, the environment of mutual understanding upon which communication is founded serves to counteract some of the influences of coercive power.

Thus, Habermas' theory can be interpreted to mean that people can challenge power and overcome its distortions by "redefining reality."[1] When I say that social actors can redefine reality, I do not mean that they can wish the world away whenever they choose. The third face of power is exercised through the manipulation of individuals' conscious interests. As such, the third face of power constructs a bounded reality for people by limiting their cognitive field of interests to the pursuit of those things that contribute to the reproduction of existing power structures. Once again, radical power instills "tastes" (Bourdieu, 1984; McGettigan, 1999; Ritzer, 2000a) for activities and commodities (e.g., automobiles, televisions, McDonald's hamburgers, etc.) that enlist enthusiastic participation in the reconstruction of hegemonic

---

[1] While, for Habermas, generating truth is tied to a social, intersubjective process, I suggest that the production of truth is an individual accomplishment. I argue that actors may demonstrate their agency when, upon perceiving evidence that is in discord with their understanding of reality, they refashion their comprehension of reality to facilitate an understanding of that discordant evidence. Acquiring knowledge that might conflict with views that are already present in the minds of agents can be accomplished by participating in communication environments, through solitary reflection, or through various encounters with the empirical world (e.g., having an apple fall on one's head). The impetus (i.e., communication, reflection, or encounters with the physical universe) that impel actors to redefine reality is not as critical to the process of generating truth as is the ability of actors to perceive phenomena of which they have had no prior conception and then to reconstruct their view of reality to accommodate their newly realized perceptions.

regimes. However, as far-reaching as ideological (Lemert, 1999; Mannheim, 1936) controls may be, they do not utterly imprison individuals.

Despite the extensive control that ideological systems exert over the minds of people, there are occasions when ideological explanatory schemes become inadequate. In some instances, the reality that is defined by an ideological system must confront phenomena that are not well explained--and that may be directly contradictory to--the principal assumptions of that ideology, e.g., the threat to the Catholic Church posed by Galileo's observation that objects orbited heavenly bodies other than the earth. While people may be encouraged (Foucault, 1977, 1980) in a variety of overt and subtle ways to maintain their faith in the reality that is propagated by established power structures, it remains within the capacity of individuals to do otherwise.

Whereas many people might remain untroubled by anomalies that are not well rationalized by established belief systems--indeed, some might be encouraged by such challenges to redouble their allegiances to besieged paradigms (Kuhn, 1970)--occasionally some individuals decide to remedy the disjunctures between their expectations versus their perceptions of reality (e.g., layers of fossils that retreat further back into time than the Biblical Creation story can account for) by "redefining reality." In other words, the limitations of established explanations for anomalous phenomena sometimes require individuals to transcend and replace those inadequate schemes with more satisfactory explanations, e.g., rather than being Created, Darwin argued that a preponderance of the available evidence indicates that species emerged out of long term struggles for survival.

Thus, redefining reality is the process through which individuals can challenge and negate some of the influences that the third face of power exercises over their consciousness; redefining reality is a means by which individuals can alter the existing landscape of social reality by creating "spaces" within which they can think and act with a degree of independence from individual, organizational, and cultural social constraints.[1] In the process of attempting to make sense of anomalies individuals tend to deconstruct (Derrida, 1978) the conceptual frameworks that limit their ability to comprehend mysterious phenomena. As individuals re-evaluate their beliefs with respect to their inability to comprehend anomalies, the features of their belief systems that do not hold up under scrutiny can be rejected. If individuals are persistent enough, they may reach a point at which the critical mass of their contemplations overwhelms the remaining shackles of their former beliefs and, thus, they may experience a "moment of truth."

A "moment of truth" is an experience wherein individuals are transported from an inadequate definition of reality to a more satisfactory version. These experiences may be considered relatively truthful moments in that they are generated through a process that involves the negation of ideological controls over an individual's definition of reality. This is

---

[1] For example, individuals who raise doubts about religious teachings are likely to encounter coercive opposition at the individual level (from scolding parents, teachers, and ministers or priests), at the organizational level (from churches or schools that zealously advocate faith in order quash doubt), and at the cultural level (in the form of religious ideology or dogma that postulates the "order" of the universe and delimits the range of aberrant vs. acceptable thought and behavior). Thus, challenging the status quo generally implies the threat of repercussions from multiple levels of authority--and, therefore, this helps to explain why individuals are often hesitant to challenge the status quo--yet, in spite of such weighty opposition, it remains possible (albeit dangerous) for determined agents to challenge all three levels of authority simultaneously.

not to say that the redefined system of beliefs at which one arrives after experiencing a moment of truth is, therefore, Truth.[1] Far from that, I argue that, in keeping with the definition of the third face of power, all established belief systems exert their own forms of radical power upon the construction of knowledge. Thus, to experience an epiphany does not transport one to an ideal realm wherein truth reigns unchallenged--as opposed to the assertions of Habermas (1970, 1972, 1981). Instead, I merely suggest that the process of redefining reality permits individuals to negate some of the influences of radical power and, thereby, negotiate with the pervasive, consciousness-distorting influences of radical power. While individuals are not capable of total emancipation, nevertheless, the capacity to redefine reality and, thereby, ascertain moments of truth implies that it is possible for individuals to create bounded spaces within a context of coercive social constraint, and, therein, grasp some awareness of their real interests.

Emancipation within Limits

Idealized versions of emancipation (Habermas, 1980; Marx and Engels, 1902), as Weber (1968) observed shrewdly, tend to be illusions at best, and nightmares at worst (Ulam, 1989). However, the despite the failure of ill-conceived political experiments, I maintain that that a specific form of emancipation remains possible even from within the confines of the most repressive regimes. The existence of a capacity for redefining reality confirms that individuals who are situated within rigid contexts of social control can emancipate themselves sufficiently to think and act in a self-determined manner. Of course, the range of such emancipation is rather limited. Once again, just because individuals can conjure novel ideas does not mean that oppressive ideological superstructures will blow away like dust in the wind. Ideological systems have quite a bit of resiliency, and their advocates know how to fight (Sobel, 1999). Nevertheless, the fact that individuals can exercise any degree of freedom within the context of social structural determination establishes grounds to assert that not only can the paradox of emancipation be solved, but also that the source and location of human agency can be specified.

The capacity to redefine reality implies that individuals are inventive, creative, ingenious, etc., enough to develop explanations that no social system, nor any living person has ever conceived previously and then apply their novel ideas to improve understanding of ill-defined phenomena, e.g., far from being "designed" to lie at the center of the universe, the earth appears to be an unplanned outcome of an ancient and mysterious cosmic cataclysm. Thus, one can view such creativity as the spark of human agency. However, agency involves more than just producing novel ideas; agency implies that humans can translate their inventive,

---

[1] Whereas Habermas suggests that the product of intersubjective communication is an ideal speech situation (i.e., during the course of communication the distortions of power will be slowly reduced until they are completely neutralized), my argument is that it is in the inception of communication--which is only sometimes followed by a limited redefinition of the reality--that actors demonstrate their capacity for agency. However, once communication has been established, because intersubjectivity must be embedded so deeply in elaborate social rules of engagement, actors cannot help but rely on social structures to sustain their interactions. Therefore, rather than developing into an environment that increasingly rejects social structural coercion and distortion, the agency that is demonstrated in the conception of communication generally becomes interwoven and more deeply embedded within the social structures that it initially challenged. Thus, rather than undoing social structures, agency is very often the mechanism through which elaborate structures of social control are transformed and extended.

unheard-of ideas into action--and in so doing, initiate social change at the individual, organizational, and sometimes even the societal level.

Powerful as social definitions of reality may be, individuals can sometimes challenge, eliminate, and replace them. For example, despite being told from birth that the earth is flat, we might observe the disturbing and unaccountable behavior of ocean-going vessels at the horizon's edge: disappearing and reappearing without being destroyed. Some observers might ignore the anomaly, or even contrive a convenient explanation that, while stretching credulity to the limit, remains consistent with what is already "known," e.g., the ships are, in fact, falling off the edge of the planet, but they are recovered from certain destruction by winged marine steeds. Alternately, more independent thinkers might treat such a dilemma as an opportunity to transcend the socially imposed barriers that constrain their comprehension of observable reality. The process of transcending socially imposed barriers begins with creative observation (e.g., "Hey! Those ships look like they are gradually slipping below the horizon") that is followed up by an individual-level challenge to social power (i.e., I guess that must mean that the horizon is not really the "end of the world"), and then the active dismantling of restrictive social controls (i.e., Based upon what I have observed, I no longer believe the earth is flat). Finally, the realization of a redefined reality involves the implementation of an entirely new explanation that simultaneously explodes existing ideological boundaries and that also provides a more adequate description of the phenomena in question, i.e., the earth's surface appears to be curved and may, in fact, be a ball zooming through space. Thus, as this example points out, individuals[1] occasionally demonstrate the requisite mental apparatus to make note of anomalies, develop creative new explanations for mysterious phenomena, and then overcome manifestations of social power that delimit thought and action. Therefore, individuals are not simply the objects of social coercion; sometimes agents can reverse the direction of such coercion and, thereby, modify themselves and the nature of the social world of which they are a part: human habits and culture all over the globe have been modified steadily ever since the postulation that the earth is spherical.

Therefore, the autonomy that individuals exercise through the process of redefining reality establishes the necessary criteria for resolving both snares of the paradox of emancipation: 1. People must define for themselves what their real interests are; 2. People can do so in real social contexts by engaging their agency to generate autonomous "spaces" within the context of social coercion that are sufficient to counteract the social forces that limit free thought. Thus, autonomy can serve as a counterfactual to identify the third face of power, precisely because it is through the exercise of agency (i.e., autonomy in the face of, and within the context of social structural coercion that occasionally produces moments of truth) that individuals are able to recognize and renegotiate the influences of the third face of power. Moments of truth are both the medium and evidence of the individual-level capacity to identify the invisible dimensions of power: via the process of redefining reality, agents can emancipate themselves sufficiently to "see" the constraints of radical power on their consciousness. Also, the autonomy that individuals generate in the process of redefining reality offers an observable counterpoint to the pervasive social control in which individuals are otherwise immersed.

---

[1] The category of "individuals" includes not just scientific geniuses, but every person with sufficient gray matter, education, and motivation to puzzle over and posit new explanations for anomalies. In other words, this means that just about everyone can and does redefine reality and, thereby, has a demonstrable capacity for agency.

Of course, the kind of autonomy that emerges from the process of redefining reality has limited degrees of freedom. While it is a noteworthy achievement for individuals to identify, eliminate, and replace inadequate explanatory constructs that define their social reality, most social actors devote the greater part of their time to laboriously reconstructing the status quo. Indeed, even agents who are involved in the process of redefining reality also tend to be engaged simultaneously in efforts to sustain the frameworks of their culture. Galileo, Einstein, Darwin, and numerous other radicals have concocted their uniquely revolutionary ideas while laboring to preserve the balance of their culture, i.e., eating the same food, wearing the same clothing, and speaking the same language both before and after the publication of their reality-reconstructing manifestos. Thus, the scope of autonomy exercised by even the most groundbreaking radicals is necessarily very narrow. Agents can exercise enough freedom to effect a little bit of social change, but then they devote 99.9% of their remaining energy toward re-embedding themselves and their ideas into a slightly modified social world.

As such, even the most ardent truth-seekers tend to spend the vast majority of their time submerged within and extending the terrain of culturally biased, "ideological" knowledge. Again, this is not the case simply because scientists are all a bunch of pampered, hypocritical apologists for reigning political regimes (although some may be). Instead, the behavior of truth-seekers needs to be understood in relation to the toil of human survival: cultural contexts equip their members with the knowledge, skills, and training necessary to survive in a competitive and sometimes cruel world. However, as Habermas (1970, p. 367) points out, it is not until humans have mastered the necessary social skills that they can competently take part in the pursuit of truth. In other words, those who never learn to read, have little chance of transcending established boundaries of knowledge, and, thus, tend to be inescapably circumscribed and manipulated by the frameworks of invisible power. However, those who are able to "master the necessary skills and competencies" may, through a process of arduous, complex and sophisticated struggles, transcend the established frameworks of cultural power, achieve a limited form of emancipation and, thereby, glimpse moments of truth. However, having achieved such emancipation, truth-seekers must endeavor, so to speak, to mend the social fabric that their landmark achievement has rent: agents must reconstruct a "constraining" social world within which lies the only feasible means of enjoying a meaningful, secure existence.

Thus, the capacity to redefine reality implies that it is possible for social scientists to identify and analyze exercises of the third face of power from within the coercive context of empirical social reality. Indeed, far from dissolving practical reality, as Habermas argues, the capacity for social actors to redefine reality implies that "good scientists" can only obtain a thorough understanding of sociological subject matter by acting as agents who interrogate the coercive context of social reality from within (McGettigan, 1997, 1999, 2001a). One must directly confront the invisible influences of social power in order to effectively grasp the complexities of the simultaneously contradictory and complimentary relationships between agents and social environments.

Redefining "Good Science"

Dahl (1957) advanced a constrained definition of power in order to avoid debates about the nature and practice of social science that broadened definitions of power can incite (Alford and Friedland, 1985). While broader definitions of power have added to the proliferation of disciplinary debates, one cannot justify the artificial constraint of sociological subject matter purely for the sake of convenience. Despite the difficulties that it creates for the definition and practice of social science, a comprehensive description of social power requires the incorporation of empirical subject matter that lie outside conventional boundaries of the observable. Just as it is illegitimate for Habermas to propose an alternative reality (i.e., ideal speech environment) to accommodate the consequences of his theoretical assertions, so too is it unacceptable to ignore vast dimensions of social reality in order to extend the longevity of an inadequate scientific paradigm. If science is to be a pursuit that genuinely seeks truthful knowledge about the empirical world, then the definition and methods of sociology must be dictated by the special requirements of its multi-dimensional subject matter.

While the production of valid scientific knowledge relies upon adequate definitions of disciplinary subject matter and appropriate research methodologies, it is also essential to generate a philosophical framework within which one's pursuit of knowledge makes sense (Wright, 1992). For example, while some lament the lack of theoretical unity in sociology (Turner and Turner, 1990), the rationale for such disunity is easy to understand. Heavy-handed attempts at theoretical unification have fallen into disrepute (Parsons, 1970) due to, among other things, their tendency to elide dissent (Lemert, 1991, 1999; Seidman, 1991). Theoretical unification implies that a single version of "The Truth" must serve for all, but which version will suffice? Brilliantly conceived as they may be, the grand theories of sociology's greatest thinkers (Addams, 1902; Bourdieu, 1984; Durkheim, 1964; Giddens, 1984; Martineau, 1834; Marx, 1906; Weber, 1968; etc.) offer only imperfect representations of the entire social landscape. Indeed, how could the viewpoint of any isolated individual be otherwise?

The notion of "redefinable reality" posits that there is a universe "out there" that exists independently of human cognition. As such, I argue that "universal truth" does exist, but such truth is not contained within existing scientific theories of the universe. Rather, "The Truth" extends infinitely into the unlocked mysteries of the expanding universe. In other words, reality is what it is: an asteroid is an asteroid is an asteroid, etc... "Truth" is an intrinsic, inseparable feature of phenomena as they exist independent of human perception. Lies and distortions come into existence via the vast human capacity for ignorance: humans view the illimitable universe through awed and flawed psyches. Thus, realization of the ultimate, universal "Truth" is only possible through a process of transitioning from inadequate to increasingly improved-- but never perfect--descriptions of the universe. Although admirable in many ways, our grasp of infinite mysteries remains woefully limited. Nevertheless, the process of redefining reality permits admittedly limited human minds to generate "moments of truth." Therefore, humans have at their disposal the necessary cognitive mechanism, i.e., moments of truth, through which to take gradual but confident steps toward a broader understanding of the infinite truths that govern the universe--and, unless I am much mistaken, that remains the explicit primary goal of the scientific enterprise.

Still, as Lukes (1974, 2005) argues, the social process of unifying knowledge claims tends to involve mechanisms that distort rather than clarify the thinking process. Imposing a single perspective on all social observers might well produce consensus, but never truth. While pessimists often conclude that this fact consigns sociological theory unavoidably to epistemological fragmentation--indeed, according to some theories (Clough, 1992, 1994; Denzin, 1997; Lather, 1991, 1993, 1995; Lemert, 1991, 1999; Lyotard, 1984; Richardson, 1991, 1994, 1995, 1996) the elimination of coherent knowledge standards represents a worthwhile achievement in itself--better meta-theoretical (Ritzer, 2000b) alternatives exist.

The version of "redefined truth" that I advocate asserts that no single perspective will ever produce a single, timeless, orthodox Truth. Instead, humans can access narrow, momentary glimpses of truth through the process of transitioning from outmoded to improved definitions of reality. As scientists (and private citizens) it is essential to embrace coherent truth standards in order to attack "bad" ideas and replace with them with "better" ideas. In denying the existence of, or requirements for, such standards, one foregoes any rational basis upon which to rebuke quacks, e.g., tyrants who would proclaim that "inferior" people should be exterminated, vigilantes who claim the right to identify and persecute "witches," barstool physicists who profess to know more about relativity than Einstein, or sociologists who contend that all forms of knowledge are equal. Redefined truth offers a basis upon which to rebuke such nonsense because limited, deceitful, or otherwise distorted explanatory schemes tend to generate a greater number of anomalies than more truthful knowledge claims, e.g., this is the primary reason that there are no departments of alchemy at accredited universities.

Still, according to the terms under which redefined truth is established, it remains up to each observer to evaluate the veracity of knowledge claims. For example, even the most widely accepted scientific theories are, and should be, subjected to intense criticism (Behe, 1996). An environment that invites criticism of even the most popular theories--whether or not we share dissenters' viewpoints--is crucial to the process of progressively and legitimately redefining truth. In other words, dissent is an acid test through which to evaluate good ideas and obliterate bad ones. Once again, no theory either has, or is ever likely to capture "the Entire Truth." Indeed, precisely because of that limitation, the notion of redefined truth is an essential means through which to emphasize that even relatively truthful ideas often can and should be supplanted by better ideas, e.g., if humans were meant to fly, they would have been born with wings vs. the Wright brothers' contention that vehicles could be developed to overcome that shortcoming. There may yet be disbelievers, but, for good, "truthful," scientific reasons, they are a marginalized minority.

Redefined truth is sure to remain unappealing to those who dream of propagating a single, unifying social and/or scientific ideology. Nevertheless, redefined truth offers a meta-theoretical means to build bridges and generate real improvements in the contemporary field of sociological theory. That is, the notion of refined truth establishes that it is possible for advocates of various theoretical perspectives to collaborate and compromise. For example, from my redefined perspective, I feel perfectly secure in stating that, despite their irreconcilable theoretical differences, Karl Marx and Max Weber were both brilliant theorists who managed to capture exceedingly valuable insights about the social world they analyzed. Neither theorist was entirely correct nor, I believe, should anyone feel conflicted about drawing upon the strengths of each theory, and ruthlessly attacking their weaknesses in an effort to develop newer, better social theories. Thus, I maintain that redefined truth makes it possible to draw constructively on the strengths of the vast storehouse of existing sociological knowledge in order to create, step-by-step, newer and better definitions of social reality. No definition of truth can legitimately claim to offer more, nor should be equipped to accomplish less.

Building Bridges

Dahl maintained that it was necessary to rely upon observable empirical events as referents for verification and evaluation of knowledge. In other words, Dahl argued that the relative "truthfulness" and thus the scientific merit of knowledge could only be evaluated with respect to a fixed (i.e., an empirically observable) standard. By arguing that there are additional invisible dimensions of power, Lukes proposed that Dahl's fixed points of observable evaluation were themselves embedded within environmental structures that served to bias the "truthful" evaluations they were intended to render. A realization of the biases that are inherent in fixed truth standards is also a fundamental component of the postmodern critique of modernist science (Lyotard 1988; Lemert 1991, 1999; Seidman 1991). Postmodernists suggest that within the very structure of unitary standards there operates a dynamic that simultaneously corrupts truth. Whereas, for truth to have any validity, it must be a standard that is consistent at all times and places; it must offer a fixed point to which knowledge may be brought for uniform and meaningful evaluation. However, the act of establishing a fixed point produces the result of, prior even to the moment of evaluation, privileging certain types of knowledge and marginalizing others. Therefore, rather than enhancing the production and accumulation of more truthful knowledge, fixed standards generally serve to legitimate the arbitrary biases that reproduce systems of cultural destructiveness and inequality (Collins 1991; Smith 1990; Wright 1992).

While the postmodern critique highlights a serious contradiction within the philosophy of modernist science, at the same time postmodernism suffers from a seemingly paradoxical contradiction of its own. The postmodernist contradiction is very similar to the paradox that Lukes encountered in positing the existence of the third face of power: due to the exercise of coercive power that appeared to be implied in standardizing the definition of real interests, he was unable to propose a consistent means with which to identify radical power. In turn, postmodern theorists have argued that modernist science subverts the pursuit of truth, but, due to their contention that standards invariably legitimate cultural biases, postmodernism never developed beyond a nihilistic critique (Lochner, 1999; McGettigan, 2000).

As a compromise, a number of theorists have advanced alternative epistemologies that are based upon localized, situated, or subjugated knowledges (Collins 1991, 1997; Denzin, 1997; Seidman 1991; Smith 1991, 1996). However, the problem that these alternatives confront is precisely the same as the dilemma Lukes encountered when he suggested that pervasive, radical power could only be identified situationally. Even though one may acknowledge that power is exercised through the imposition of universal standards, it is not tenable epistemologically to abandon universal knowledge claims. To sustain the claim that radical power is pervasive, one must identify a universal standard with which to recognize its effects consistently. The deeper issue that advocates of particularistic epistemologies must contend with is: how is it possible to identify a standard of truth that can identify exercises of radical power--and, thereby, a coherent alternative to conventional "good science"--but that also avoids being corrupted by such power? Here again, a solution may be derived from the concept of autonomy.

Defining exercises of radical power in terms of autonomy implies that truth can only emerge when the distortions of coercive power are negated. Thus, the concept of autonomy offers a standard of truth that avoids the inherent biases of other fixed points. Rather than imposing a homogenizing truth standard, autonomy implies that it is only through particularized efforts to challenge coercion that increasingly undistorted forms of knowledge can be achieved.

Thus, redefined truth can help resolve the epistemological dilemmas that are faced by advocates of particularistic alternatives to conventional science by offering a fixed point that promotes, rather than disqualifies, a consideration of the localized experiences of social actors (McGettigan, 1999, 2000, 2001a). Redefined truth also implies that, although individual social actors may be inextricably submerged in and dependent upon complex social environments, individuals can recognize, and in a limited way, challenge the imposition of social constraint. Indeed, redefined truth is contingent upon the capacity that social actors' have to transform their view of reality independently of, and in opposition to, the influences of their social environments. While this does not imply that all social scientists must be political activists, this does indicate that one must often challenge the status quo in order to avoid being befuddled by it (McGettigan, 1999, 2001a). Once again, moments of truth are necessarily a product of individual-level challenges to social constraints; the social structures that we study are often a significant impediment to realizing truth. Indeed, shedding light on the structure of social power tends to "expose" issues that the dynamics of social power are designed to shroud (Chomsky, 1996; Domhoff, 2002; Mills, 1956). Thus, the simple act of studying social power implies that one must be prepared to challenge the status quo, "contaminate" (Richardson, 1994) the environment under observation, and stimulate the potential for social change (McGettigan 1999, 2001a).

Despite Durkheim's (1965) protestations to the contrary, no social facts are sacred. Sometimes, to understand the social world, we need to alter it, and if doing so implies an assault on various manifestations of social blight and injustice, then so be it (Du Bois, 1997; Durkheim, 1966; Fleuhr-Lobban, 1995; Friedan, 1964; Herman and Chomsky, 1995; hooks, 1994; Marx and Engels, 1902; McGettigan, 1997, 2001a, 2001b; Orwell, 1984; Wolf, 1991).

Therefore, a redefined view of truth implies that for anyone--including social scientists--to grasp the nature of social reality, they must exercise their capacity as situated social agents to challenge and more clearly perceive the invisible influences that interact with situated social agents in the process of reproducing the structure of social environments; it is only through such active engagements that "moments of truth" can emerge (McGettigan, 1997, 1999, 2000, 2001a). In this way, the definition of "good science" can be broadened to assert that, rather than constraining the scope of social subject matter, more truthful knowledge can only be obtained through the active efforts of situated social actors to overcome the limitations that confine their understanding of empirical social reality.

Conclusion

The goal of "good scientists" was to transform the sociology of philosophical debate into one of sound, conventional science. However, whether one wishes to engage in philosophical debates or not, there are philosophical implications associated with every definition of science. The conventional definition of science, despite its adherents' commitment to objectivity, is tied to an overly simplistic definition of power and sociological subject matter. A redefined approach to science can conceptualize additional dimensions of power: recognizing the influence that power has over the behavior of social actors, the minds of "objective" observers and the substance of empirical reality.

Additionally, adopting a redefined orientation to truth enables researchers to conceptualize the seemingly paradoxical relationship between actors, agency, and social structure. By endeavoring to produce knowledge that acknowledges and respects individual perspectives, it becomes possible to better appreciate the ways that power affects knowledge and the process through which actors may simultaneously experience the generation of agency and thoroughly understand the multi-dimensional fabrication of society.

References

Addams, Jane, 1902. *Democracy and Social Ethics*. New York: Macmillan Co.

Alexander, Jeffrey C. (Ed.), 1987. *The Micro-Macro Link*. Berkeley: University of California Press.

Alford, Robert R., and Roger Friedland, 1985. *Powers of Theory: Capitalism, the State, and Democracy*. New York: Cambridge University Press.

Arendt, Hannah, 1969. *On Violence*. New York: Harcourt Brace Jovanovich.

Bachrach, Peter, and Morton S. Baratz, 1963. "Decisions and Non-Decisions: An Analytical Framework." *American Political Science Review* 57: 641-651.

Bachrach, Peter, and Morton S. Baratz, 1970. *Power and Poverty: Theory and Practice*. Oxford: Oxford University Press.

Behe, Michael J., 1996. *Darwin's Black Box : The Biochemical Challenge to Evolution*. New York. Free Press.

Benton, Ted, 1981. "'Objective' Interests and the Sociology of Power." *Sociology* 15 (2): 161-184.

Bourdieu, Piere, 1984. *Distinction: A Social Critique of the Judgment of Taste*. (Translated by Richard Nice.) Cambridge, Mass.: Harvard University Press.

Bradshaw, A, 1976. "A Critique of Steven Lukes' 'Power: A Radical View.'" *Sociology* 10: 121-127.

Burawoy, Michael, 1979. *Manufacturing Consent: Changes in the Labor Process Under Monopoly Capitalism*. Chicago: University of Chicago Press.

Chomsky, Noam, 1996. *World Orders Old and New*. New York: Columbia University Press.

Clegg, Stewart R. 1989. *Frameworks of Power*. London: Sage.

Clough, Patricia Ticineto, 1992. *The End(s) of Ethnography: From Realism to Social Criticism*. Newbury Park: Sage.

Clough, Patricia Ticineto, 1994. *Feminist Thought: Desire, Power and Academic Discourse*. Cambridge, MA: Blackwell.

Collins, Patricia Hill, 1991. *Black Feminist Thought: Knowledge, Consciousness and the Politics of Empowerment*. New York: Routledge.

Collins, Patricia Hill, 1997. "How Much Difference is Too Much: Black Feminist Thought and the Politics of Postmodern Social Theory." *Current Perspectives in Social Theory* 17: 3-37.

Dahl, Robert A. 1957. "The Concept of Power." *Behavioural Science* 2: 201-205.

Dahl, Robert A. 1961. *Who Governs? Democracy and Power in an American City*. New Haven: Yale University Press.

Denzin, Norman K. 1997. "The Standpoint Epistemologies and Social Theory." *Current Perspectives in Social Theory* 17: 39-76.

Derrida, Jacques, 1978. *Writing and Difference*. (Translated by Alan Bass). Chicago: University of Chicago Press.

Domhoff, G. William, 2002. *Who Rules America?: Power and Politics*. 4th ed. Boston: McGraw Hill.

Du Bois, W. E. B., 1997. *The Souls of Black Folk*. Las Vegas, NV: Classic Americana.

Durkheim, Emile, 1964. *The Division of Labor in Society*. (Translated by George Simpson.) New York: Free Press of Glencoe.

Durkheim, Emile, 1965. *The Elementary forms of Religious Life*. New York: Free Press.

Durkheim, Emile, 1966. *Suicide*. New York: Free Press.

Fleuhr-Lobban, Carolyn, 1995. "Cultural Relativism and Universal Rights." *The Chronicle of Higher Education.* 41: 39 (June 9) B1-B2.

Foucault, Michel, 1977. *Discipline and Punish: The Birth of the Prison.* (Translated by Alan Sheridan.) New York: Pantheon Books.

Foucault, Michel, 1980. *Power/Knowledge: Selected Interviews and Other Writings 1972-1977.* Edited by Colin Gordon. New York: Pantheon Books.

Friedan, Betty, 1964. *The Feminine Mystique.* New York: Dell.

Gaventa, John, 1980. *Power and Powerlessness: Quiescence and Rebellion in and Appalachian Valley.* Urbana: University of Illinois Press.

Giddens, Anthony, 1984. *The Constitution of Society: Outline of the Theory of Structuration.* Berkeley: UC Press.

Gould, Stephen Jay, 1996. *The Mismeasure of Man.* New York: Norton.

Gramsci, Antonio, 1992. *Prison Notebooks.* (Edited by Joseph A. Buttigieg. Translated by Joseph A. Buttigieg and Antonio Callari). New York: Columbia University Press.

Habermas, Jürgen, 1970. "Toward a Theory of Communicative Competence." *Inquiry* 13: 360-365.

Habermas, Jürgen, 1972. *Knowledge and Human Interests.* London: Heinemann Educational Books.

Habermas, Jürgen, 1981. *Theory of Communicative Action.* 2 vols. London: Heinemann. Vol. 1, *Reason and the Rationalization of Society*, also published by Polity Press, Cambridge, England, 1984.

Herman, Edward S., and Noam Chomsky, 1995. *Manufacturing Consent: The Political Economy of the Mass Media.* London: Vintage/Ebury.

hooks, bell, 1994. *Outlaw Culture. Resisting Representations.* New York: Routledge.

Isaac, Jeffrey C. 1987. *Power and Marxist Theory: A Realist View.* Ithaca: Cornell University Press.

Kernohan, Andrew, 1989. "Social Power and Human Agency." *The Journal of Philosophy* 86: 12 (December) 712-726.

Kuhn, Thomas S., 1970. *The Structure of Scientific Revolutions.* Chicago: University of Chicago Press.

Lather, Patti, 1991. *Getting Smart: Feminist Research and Pedagogy With/in the Postmodern.* New York: Routledge.

Lather, Patti, 1993. "Fertile Obsession: Validity After Poststructuralism." *The Sociological Quarterly* 34: (4) 673-693.

Lather, Patti, 1995. "The Validity of Angels: Interpretive and Textual Strategies in Researching the Lives of Women With HIV/AIDS." *Qualitative Inquiry* 1: (1) 41-68.

Lemert, Charles, 1991. "The End of Ideology, Really." *Sociological Theory* 9: 164-172.

Lemert, Charles (ed.), 1999. *Social Theory: The Multicultural and Classic Readings.* 2nd Edition. Boulder: Westview Press.

Lochner, David, 1999. "Unacknowledged Roots and Blatant Imitation: Postmodernism and the Dada Movement." *Electronic Journal of Sociology* 4: (1). http://www.sociology.org/content/vol004.001/locher.html

Lukes, Steven, 1982. "Of Gods and Demons: Habermas and Practical Reason." Pp. 134-148 in *Habermas: Critical Debates.* Edited by John B. Thompson and David Held. Cambridge: The MIT Press.

Lukes, Steven, 2005. *Power: A Radical View.* Second Edition. London: Palgrave Macmillan.

Lyotard, Jean-Francois, 1984. *The Postmodern Condition: A Report on Knowledge.* (Translated by Geoff Bennington and Brian Massumi) Minneapolis: University of Minnesota Press.

Mann, Michael, 1986. *The Sources of Social Power, Vol. 1: A History of Power from the Beginning to A.D. 1760*. Cambridge: Cambridge University Press.

Mannheim, Karl, 1936. *Ideology and Utopia: An Introduction to the Sociology of Knowledge.* (Translated by Louis Wirth and Edward Shils.) New York: Harcourt, Brace, Jovanovich.

Martineau, Harriet, 1834. *Illustrations of Political Economy*. London: C. Fox.

Marx, Karl, 1906. *Capital: A Critique of Political Economy*. Chicago, C.H. Kerr & Company, 1906-09.

Marx, Karl and Frederick Engels, 1902. *Manifesto of the Communist Party*. (Authorized English translation edited and annotated by Frederick Engels.) Chicago: C. H. Kerr & Company.

McGettigan, Timothy, 1998. "Redefining Reality: Epiphany as a Standard of Postmodern Truth." Published in the *Electronic Journal of Sociology* 3 (4). http://www.sociology.org/content/vol003.004/mcgettigan.html

McGettigan, Timothy, 1999. *Utopia on Wheels: Blundering Down the Road to Reality.* Lanham, MD.: University Press of America.

McGettigan, Timothy, 2000. "Flawed by Design: The Virtues and Limitations of Postmodern Theory." Published in *Theory & Science* 1 (1). http://theoryandscience.icaap.org/content/vol001.001/05mcgettigan.html

McGettigan, Timothy, 2001a. "Field Research for Boneheads: From Naïveté to Insight on the Green Tortoise." *Sociological Research Online* 6 (2). http://www.socresonline.org.uk/6/2/mcgettigan.html

McGettigan, Timothy, 2001b. Caveat Emptor: A Market for Conquest. *Globalization*, 1 (1). http://globalization.icaap.org/content/v1.1/editor.html

Mead, George Herbert, 1934. *Mind, Self and Society*. Chicago: University of Chicago Press.

Mills, C. Wright, 1956. *The Power Elite*. Oxford: Oxford University Press.

Mill, C. Wright, 1959. *The Sociological Imagination*. New York: Oxford University Press.

Orwell, George, 1983. *1984: A Novel*. New York: New American Library.

Parsons, Talcott, 1960. "The Distribution of Power in American Society." In *Structure and Process in American Societies*. New York: The Free Press.

Parsons, Talcott, 1978. *Action Theory and the Human Condition*. New York: Free Press.

Popper, Karl R., 1959. *The Logic of Scientific Discovery*. New York: Harper Torchbooks.

Richardson, Laurel, 1991. "Postmodern Social Theory: Representational Practices." *Sociological Theory* 9: 2 (Fall) 173-179.

Richardson, Laurel, 1994. "Writing: A Method of Inquiry." Pp. 516-529 in *Handbook of Qualitative Research*. Norman K. Denzin and Yvonna S. Lincoln (Eds.). Thousand Oaks, CA: Sage.

Richardson, Laurel, 1995. "Co-Authoring 'The Sea Monster,' a Writing Story." *Qualitative Inquiry* (1) 2: 189-203.

Richardson, Laurel, 1996. "A Sociology of Responsibility." *Qualitative Sociology* 19: (4) 519-524.

Richardson, Laurel, 1998. "Meta-Jeopardy." *Qualitative Inquiry* (4) 4: 464-468.

Ritzer, George, 2000a. *The McDonaldization of Society*. New Century Edition. Thousand Oaks, CA: Pine Forge Press.

Ritzer, George, 2000b. *Sociological Theory*. Fifth Edition. New York: McGraw Hill.

Schlosser, Eric, 2001. *Fast Food Nation: The Dark Side of the All-American Meal*. Boston: Houghton Mifflin.

Smith, Dorothy, 1990. *The Conceptual Practices of Power: A Feminist Sociology of Knowledge*. London: Routledge.

Smith, Dorothy, 1992. "Sociology from Women's Experience: A Reaffirmation." *Sociological Theory* 10: 1 (Spring) 88-98.

Smith, Dorothy E., 1996. "Telling the Truth After Postmodernism." *Symbolic Interaction* 19: 171-202.

Sobel, Dava, 1999. *Galileo's Daughter: A Historical Memoir of Science, Faith, and Love*. New York: Walker & Co.

Turner, Jonathan, 1987. "Analytical Theorizing." Pp. 156-194 in Social Theory Today edited by A. Giddens, and J. Turner. 1987. Stanford: Stanford University Press.

Turner, Stephen Park, and Jonathan H. Turner, 1990. *The Impossible Science : An Institutional Analysis of American Sociology*. Newbury Park, CA.: Sage Publications.

Ulam, Adam B., 1989. *Stalin: The Man and His Era*. Boston: Beacon Press, 1989.

Wartenberg, Thomas E. 1990. *The Forms of Power: From Domination to Transformation*. Philadelphia: Temple University Press.

Weber, Max, 1968. *Economy and Society: An Outline of Interpretive Sociology*. (Edited by Guenther Roth and Claus Wittich. Translators: Ephraim Fischoff, et al. New York: Bedminster Press.

Wiley, Norbert, 1994. *The Semiotic Self*. Chicago: The University of Chicago Press.

Willis, Paul, 1977. *Learning to Labor: How Working Class Kids Get Working Class Jobs*. New York: Columbia University Press.

Wolf, Naomi, 1991. *The Beauty Myth*. London: Vintage/Ebury.

Wolfe, Tom, 1968. *The Electric Kool-Aid Acid Test*. New York, Farrar, Straus and Giroux.

Wolfinger, Raymond E. 1971. "Nondecisions and the Study of Local Politics." American Political Science Review 65: 1063-1080.

Wright, Will, 1992. *Wild Knowledge: Science, Language, and Social Life in a Fragile Environment*. Minneapolis: University of Minnesota Press.

CHAPTER FOUR

Flawed by Design[1]

The Virtues and Limitation of Postmodern Theory

Abstract

Nothing is perfect in an imperfect world—especially science. The postmodern critique of Enlightenment science has driven home that point forcefully. However, despite the harshness of its critique, postmodernism has fallen well short of creating a viable alternative to modern science. In this paper, I argue that the only recourse for postmodernists is to adopt a new orientation to the fundamental pursuit of modernist science: truth.

A World of Change

Sociology and modernity have always been inextricably interrelated. As the early framers of the discipline pointed out (Addams, 1907; Comte, 1896; Durkheim 1964; Martineau, 1838; Marx, 1992; Marx and Engels, 1998; Weber, 1978), the logic of the "traditional" world, i.e., rural, agricultural, provincial, static, did not apply well to an urban, industrial, secular, global society (Durkheim, 1951; Simmel, 1971, 1978; Tönnies, 1963; Weber, 1946). Instead, a new form of forward looking—or enlightened (Ritzer, 1996)—social logic was required to make sense of a rapidly revolutionizing world and, thus, the science of society was born.

The charter of modern, enlightened science has been to generate knowledge (Ashley and Orenstein, 1998; Coser and Rosenberg, 1989; Lemert, 1999; McGettigan, 1998, 1999; McIntyre, 1999; Ritzer, 1996; Rossides, 1998; Turner, et. al., 1995). Indeed, not only has science assisted in bringing our understanding of modernity up to speed, but it has also promised to create a "better" society. The basis for such a bold assertion—which, by the way, has been voiced by theorists of widely varying stripes (Comte, 1896; Durkheim, 1964; Marx, 1992)—was that science rested on a qualitatively stronger epistemological foundation than any other belief system. Whereas other systems were regulated by established dogmas, science was (presumably) beholden to no earthly influence save the pursuit of truth, the most pristine of intellectual standards.

Philosophically speaking, the possibilities of applying science to the reconstruction of an evolving society were, to say the least, exciting. In an enlightened age, the scourge of social

---

[1]   This is an updated version of an article originally published in *Theory and Science*: http://theoryandscience.icaap.org/content/vol001.001/05mcgettigan.html

pathology would doubtlessly wither under the antiseptic light of scientific scrutiny. Further, sweeping democratic reforms promised to unite with science in a mutual struggle to uplift humanity. For it to flourish, "good science" required democratic freedoms that ensured unfettered opportunities for inquiry. In return, science promised to invigorate the public's long neglected intellect. Fueled by their reciprocal aspirations, science and democracy have indeed combined to influence profoundly the people, politics, and economics of the modern world.

Yet, despite the spectacular achievements of modernity's juggernaut (Giddens, 1990), the fabled "good society" remains far from realized. Certainly, there are many who enjoy luxurious living standards. Nevertheless, as modernity has progressed, the numbers of people living in abject poverty has also increased (McLaren, 2000; United Nations Development Programme, 1998). While some have insisted that culpability lies with those who are least fortunate (Murray, 1984, 1998; Rostow, 1960), others contend that fault lies elsewhere.

Modernity's Achilles Heel

Postmodernists have hammered hard at the illusion propagated by modernist theorists that science would ultimately generate truth and, thereby, a better world for one and all (Clough, 1992, 1994; Denzin, 1996, 1997; Kincheloe and McLaren, 1994; Lather, 1991, 1993, 1995; Lemert, 1991, 1999; Lyotard, 1984; Richardson, 1991, 1994, 1995, 1996; Seidman, 1991; Tierney, 1997). Indeed, if modernity was supposed to ameliorate social problems, then why, after approximately two hundred years of enlightening scientific development, has global misery actually *increased*? Postmodernists have a ready answer to this question: because the promises of the Enlightenment were lies.

Far from achieving the Enlightenment's philosophical goals, postmodernists maintain that science has sustained a long-standing project to exploit people everywhere (Denzin, 1997; Kincheloe and McLaren, 1994; Lather, 1995; Lemert, 1991; Seidman, 1991). In other words, the Enlightenment is a western European invention that is permeated by a variety of significant biases (e.g., patriarchy, racism, Christianity, rabid industrialism, etc.). Thus, despite pretensions of objectivity, Western cultural biases have thoroughly tainted every aspect of modern "progress" (Smith, 1990): the language, customs, and ideals of the West are emulated everywhere. Therefore, if it is a better social world that we seek, then, as postmodernists suggest, we may need to strike out along a new path. However, one need ask, after having molded the globe in the image of the West, is there any feasible alternative to juggernaut?

A Clarion Call for Inaction

In response to the evils that have been proliferated (whether intentionally or not) by the purveyors of modernist science, postmodernists have called for a "humanization" of the collective social endeavor: scientific, economic, and otherwise (Denzin, 1995, 1997; Lather, 1995; Lemert, 1999). Postmodernists have argued that the juggernaut of modernity can be challenged most effectively by rejecting every assertion that knowledge or truth is generalizable (Seidman, 1991). Therefore, where there is no truth, there can be no justification for superimposing Western values and interests; to do so would constitute an unequivocal and unacceptable act of violence.

This orientation to the philosophy of knowledge accomplishes a number of important goals for postmodernists. First, by elevating the status of "common knowledge," the arbitrary, destructive power of science can be offset. Secondly, postmodernists have argued that, as a consequence of eliminating the pre-eminence of truth standards, "learned dialogues" are likely to become populated by a greater number and diversity of voices (Lemert, 1999). Consequently, by creating an environment wherein the oppressed may give voice to their concerns, the rotten core of modernity is more likely to be exposed.

Having rejected the modernist emphasis on truth, a variety of postmodern "artistic" practices have been developed for the purpose of steering science in new directions (Brady, 1998; Janesick, 1994; L. Richardson, 1995, 1998; M. Richardson, 1998; Travisano, 1998). Yet, while there have been some noteworthy attempts to organize postmodernists around substantial scientific projects (Denzin and Lincoln, 1994, 2000), no clearly defined postmodernist plan of attack has yet emerged. Indeed, the inability of postmodernists to mount a full counteroffensive to modernism has stimulated Lochner (1999) to propose that postmodernism is simply a poorly repackaged version of Dadaism, a nihilistic artistic movement. Lochner notes that, shortly after being recognized as a definable movement in the arts, Dada's principal artists disbanded: once they had established that their movement was opposed to all forms of standardized control, there was nowhere else for Dadaists to go. Lochner even asserts that certain leading figures in the contemporary postmodern movement (Jean Baudrillard, in particular) have intentionally ignored their debt to Dadaism for two reasons:

1. This would establish that their revolutionary social theory was not, in fact, terribly original.
2. This would also indicate that there was no future for postmodernism—either in theory or practice.

Still, while the motives of some postmodernists may be rather dubious, I do not think all the goals of postmodernism should be dismissed. There are many important reasons to question and criticize the modern world. However, as the Dadaists discovered long ago, the tactic of abandoning truth is an entirely unworkable strategy (i.e., one disavows every credible basis upon which to construct or criticize knowledge). Further, it is not possible to base any sort of "movement" on such a relativistic, nihilistic epistemology. Consequently, for postmodernism to move in a more meaningful direction—a move that has been called for by others as well (Brents, 1999; Campbell, 1998; Kincheloe and McLaren, 1994; Lange, 1998; McLaren, 2000)—I believe that postmodernists must reinvigorate the roots of their critique: how is it possible to organize a more just, fair, free, equal, and democratic world? Oddly enough, these should sound like familiar questions because they are precisely the same questions posed by Enlightenment scientists.

The philosophy of Enlightenment science was forged to the presumption that the world was changing rapidly, and with the "right" kind of tinkering it could become a better place (Comte, 1896; Durkheim, 1964; Hobbes, 1969; Locke, 1947; Machiavelli, 1999; Marx and Engels, 1998; Rousseau, 1967). Postmodernists have performed the valuable service of pointing out that such tinkering has been managed by neither an exact, nor a very fair world of science. Since science has perpetrated and justified a lot of regrettable tinkering in the modern era, its task now, at the very least, should be to ensure that its worst offenses are not repeated. But how can that be accomplished?

73

Up till now, the crucial flaw in the postmodern strategy has been its unequivocal rejection of universal truth; a strategy that is roughly akin to combating foes by lopping off one's own head. If postmodernists want to impugn the claims of Enlightenment science, then they must assert a more primary definition of truth. That is, without offering a more convincing definition of "postmodern truth," then we must accept the modernist definition—if for no other reason than because modernist scientists believe in it. Thus, it is only by asserting an alternate definition of truth that postmodernists will be able to *un*do modernist science.

An Alternate Definition of Truth

I have argued elsewhere (McGettigan 1998, 1999) that truth does exist and it can be produced by anyone—not just scientists. In spite of all the ideology that has been broadcast in the modern world, it remains within the capacity of individuals to "redefine reality." In the process of redefining reality, people transform their understanding of anomalous phenomena by refuting dogma, e.g., Galileo's rejection of the earth-centered theory of the universe, or Darwin's assertion of natural selection as the motor of evolutionary history. When individuals redefine reality they do not suddenly arrive at an ideal world wherein Truth reigns supreme (Habermas 1970, 1972, 1981, 1993), but instead they realize a "moment of truth," i.e., the time frame in which they are transported from an ideologically proscribed view of the universe to a more inventive version of reality. Truth, according to this definition, may be produced by individuals who actively overcome the influences of social power that limit the boundaries of understanding.

Thus, if postmodernists are interested in criticizing science for the purposes of building a "better world," then they will need to adopt a clearly defined standard of truth. An "emergent" view of truth (McGettigan, 1998, 1999) maintains that it is essential for truth to be generated at the level of the individual. Consequently, not only is this notion of truth compatible with an epistemology that respects a multiplicity of voices, but it can also serve as a basis upon which to critique and move beyond the limitations of modernist science.

As long as postmodernists remain committed to an anti-truth orientation to science, they will be unable to overcome the inherent limitations of their epistemology. This does not mean, however, that science will be hindered in its progress. No doubt, modern science will continue to precipitate social change with admirable efficacy. Therefore, if postmodernists want to counteract such change, then they will need to develop a sound scientific strategy—which, as we learned from modernist scholars a long time ago, can only be accomplished by seeking the truth.

References

Addams, Jane, 1907. *Democracy and Social Ethics*. New York: Macmillan.

Ashley, David, and David Michael Orenstein, 1998. *Sociological Theory: Classical Statements*. Fourth Edition. Boston: Allyn and Bacon.

Brady, Ivan, 1998. "A Gift of the Journey." *Qualitative Inquiry* (4) 4: 463.

Brents, Barbara G., 1999. "Dale Carnegie, the Carpenters, and Cambodia." *Journal of Contemporary Ethnography* (27) 4: 435-460.

Campbell, David, 1998. "Why Fight: Humanitarianism, Principles, and Post-Structuralism." *Millenium* (27) 3, Winter:497-521.

Clough, Patricia Ticineto, 1992. *The End(s) of Ethnography: From Realism to Social Criticism.* Newbury Park: Sage.

Clough, Patricia Ticineto, 1994. *Feminist Thought: Desire, Power and Academic Discourse.* Cambridge, MA: Blackwell.

Comte, Auguste, 1896. *The Positive Philosophy of Auguste Comte.* (Translated and condensed by Harriet Martineau. London: G. Bell & Sons.

Coser, Lewis A., and Bernard Rosenberg, 1989. *Sociological Theory: A Book of Readings.* Fifth Edition. Prospect Heights, IL: Waveland Press.

Denzin, Norman K., 1996. "Post-Pragmatism." *Symbolic Interaction* 19 (1): 61-75.

Denzin, Norman K., 1997. "The Standpoint Epistemologies and Social Theory." *Current Perspectives in Social Theory* 17: 39-76.

Denzin, Norman K., and Yvonna S. Lincoln (eds.), 1994. *The Handbook of Qualitative Research.* Thousand Oaks, CA.: Sage.

Denzin, Norman K., and Yvonna S. Lincoln (eds.), 2000. *The Handbook of Qualitative Research. 2nd Edition.* Thousand Oaks, CA.: Sage.

Durkheim, Emile, 1951. *Suicide.* (Translated by John A. Spaulding and George Simpson). Glencoe, IL.: Free Press.

Durkheim, Emile, 1964. *The Division of Labor in Society.* (Translated by George Simpson.) New York: Free Press.

Giddens, Anthony, 1990. *The Consequences of Modernity*. Stanford: Stanford University Press.

Habermas, Jürgen, 1970. "Toward a Theory of Communicative Competence." *Inquiry* 13: 360-365.

Habermas, Jürgen, 1972. *Knowledge and Human Interests*. London: Heinemann Educational Books.

Habermas, Jürgen, 1981. *Theory of Communicative Action*. 2 vols. London: Heinemann. Vol. 1, *Reason and the Rationalization of Society*, also published by Polity Press, Cambridge, England, 1984.

Habermas, Jürgen, 1993. *Justification and Application: Remarks on Discourse Ethics*. Cambridge, MA: The MIT Press.

Hobbes, Thomas, 1969. *Leviathan*. New York: Meridian.

Janesick, Valerie J., 1994. "The Dance of Qualitative Research Design: Metaphor, Methodolatry, and Meaning." Pp. 209-219 in *Handbook of Qualitative Research*. Norman K. Denzin and Yvonna S. Lincoln (Eds.). Thousand Oaks, CA: Sage.

Kincheloe, Joe L. and Peter L. McLaren, 1994, "Rethinking Critical Theory and Qualitative Research." Pp. 138-157 in *Handbook of Qualitative Research*. Norman K. Denzin and Yvonna S. Lincoln (Eds.). Thousand Oaks, CA: Sage.

Lange, Lynda, 1998. "Burnt Offerings to Rationality: A Feminist Reading of the Construction of Indigenous Peoples in Enrique Dussel's Theory of Modernity." *Hypatia* (13) 3, Summer: 132-145

Lather, Patti, 1991. *Getting Smart: Feminist Research and Pedagogy With/in the Postmodern*. New York: Routledge.

Lather, Patti, 1993. "Fertile Obsession: Validity After Poststructuralism." *The Sociological Quarterly* 34: (4) 673-693.

Lather, Patti, 1995. "The Validity of Angels: Interpretive and Textual Strategies in Researching the Lives of Women With HIV/AIDS." *Qualitative Inquiry* 1: (1) 41-68.

Lemert, Charles, 1991. "The End of Ideology, Really." *Sociological Theory* 9: 2 (Fall) 164-172.

Lemert, Charles (ed.), 1999. *Social Theory: The Multicultural and Classic Readings*. 2nd Edition. Boulder: Westview Press.

Lochner, David, 1999. "Unacknowledged Roots and Blatant Imitation: Postmodernism and the Dada Movement." *Electronic Journal of Sociology* 4: (1).

Locke, John, 1947. *Two Treatises of Government*. New York: Hafner.

Lyotard, Jean-Francois, 1984. *The Postmodern Condition: A Report on Knowledge*. (Translated by Geoff Bennington and Brian Massumi) Minneapolis: University of Minnesota Press.

Machiavelli, Niccolo, 1999. *The Prince*. New York: Penguin.

Martineau, Harriet, 1838. *How to Observe Morals and Manners*. London: Charles Knight and Company.

Marx, Karl, 1992. *Capital: A Critique of Political Economy*. Volume I. (Translated by Ben Fowkes.) New York: Penguin.

Marx, Karl, and Friedrich Engels, 1998. *The Communist Manifesto*. New York: Signet Classic.

McGettigan, Timothy, 1998. "Redefining Reality: Epiphany as a Standard of Postmodern Truth." *Electronic Journal of Sociology* 3 (4). http://www.sociology.org/vol003.004/mcgettigan.article.1998.html

McGettigan, Timothy, 1999. *Utopia on Wheels: Blundering Down the Road to Reality*. Lanham, MD.: University Press of America.

McIntyre, Lisa J., 1999. *The Practical Skeptic: Core Concepts in Sociology*. Mountain View, CA.: Mayfield.

McLaren, Peter, 2000. *Che Guevara, Paulo Freire, and the Pedagogy of the Revolution*. Lanham, MD.: Roman and Littlefield.

Murray, Charles, 1984. *Losing Ground: American Social Policy, 1950-1980*. New York: Basic Books.

Murray, Charles, 1998. *Income Inequality and IQ*. Washington: The AEI Press.

Richardson, Laurel, 1991. "Postmodern Social Theory: Representational Practices." *Sociological Theory* 9: 2 (Fall) 173-179.

Richardson, Laurel, 1994. "Writing: A Method of Inquiry." Pp. 516-529 in *Handbook of Qualitative Research*. Norman K. Denzin and Yvonna S. Lincoln (Eds.). Thousand Oaks, CA: Sage.

Richardson, Laurel, 1995. "Co-Authoring 'The Sea Monster,' a Writing Story." *Qualitative Inquiry* (1) 2: 189-203.

Richardson, Laurel, 1996. "A Sociology of Responsibility." *Qualitative Sociology* 19: (4) 519-524.

Richardson, Laurel, 1998. "Meta-Jeopardy." *Qualitative Inquiry* (4) 4: 464-468.

Richardson, Miles, 1998. "Poetics in the Field and on the Page." *Qualitative Inquiry* (4) 4: 451-462.

Ritzer, George, 1996. *Sociological Theory*. Fourth Edition. New York: McGraw-Hill.

Rossides, Daniel W., 1998. *Social Theory: Its Origins, History, and Contemporary Relevance*. Dix Hills, N.Y.: General Hall.

Rostow, Walt W., 1960. *The Stages of Economic Growth: A Non-Communist Manifesto*. Cambridge: Cambridge University Press.

Rousseau, Jean-Jacques, 1967. *The Social Contract and Discourse on the Origin of Inequality*. New York: Pocket Books.

Seidman, Steven, 1991. "The End of Sociological Theory: The Postmodern Hope." *Sociological Theory* 9: 2 (Fall) 131-146.

Simmel, Georg, 1971. "The Metropolis and Mental Life." Pp. 324-339 in *Georg Simmel: On Individuality and Social Forms* (Translated and edited by Donald N. Levine). Chicago: University of Chicago Press.

Simmel, Georg, 1978. *The Philosophy of Money*. (Translated by Tom Bottomore and David Frisby). London: Routledge and Kegan Paul.

Smith, Dorothy E., 1990. *The Conceptual Practices of Power: A Feminist Sociology of Knowledge*. London: Routledge.

Tierney, William G., 1997. *Academic Outlaws: Queer Theory and Cultural Studies in the Academy*. Thousand Oaks, CA: Sage.

Tönnies, Ferdinand, 1963. *Gemeinschaft and Gesellschaft*. (Translated and edited by Charles P. Loomis). New York: Harper and Row.

Travisano, Richard V., 1998. "On Becoming Italian American: An Autobiography of an Ethnic Identity. *Qualitative Inquiry* (4) 4: 540-563.

Turner, Jonathan H., Leonard Beeghley, and Charles H. Powers, 1995. *The Emergence of Sociological Theory*. Third Edition. Boston: Wadsworth.

United Nations Development Programme, 1998. *Human Development Report 1998*. New York: Oxford University Press.

Weber, Max, 1946. "Science as a Vocation." Pp. 129-156 in *From Max Weber: Essays in Sociology* (Translated and Edited by H. H. Gerth and C. Wright Mills). New York: Oxford University Press.

Weber, Max, 1978. *Economy and Society: An Outline of Interpretive Sociology*. Volumes I & II. (Edited by Guenther Roth and Claus Wittich). Berkeley: University of California Press.

CHAPTER FIVE

Anomaly Overload[1]

An Evolutionary Theory of Truth

Abstract

Truth may be defined as "undistorted knowledge." Straightforward as that definition may appear, there are seemingly endless problems associated with specifying truth standards. Positivists maintain that truth must be defined with respect to empirically observable criteria. In response, power elite theorists have asserted that due to the interventions of power-brokers, observable reference points are untrustworthy. Further, postmodernists have concluded that due to the pervasive influences of cultural power, the pursuit of universal truth should be aborted. In spite of these pessimistic appraisals, this article advances an epistemology that is founded upon an "evolving" but nonetheless universal definition of truth.

Introduction

Thomas Kuhn (1970) argued that scientific revolutions take place when dominant paradigms are dislodged by emergent paradigms. Science undergoes such transitions when established paradigms fail to account for an increasing number of empirical anomalies. Anomalies may be understood as enigmas for which existing knowledge systems lack convincing explanations. Kuhn's perspective challenged the previously accepted view that the accumulation of scientific knowledge was a rational stepwise process, i.e., each landmark discovery being anticipated with logical precision and, once established, elevated consensually atop a vertical tower of knowledge. Instead, Kuhn contended that paradigm shifts are much messier undertakings that are marked by infighting, political subterfuge, and a host of other unscientific antics. In other words, though scientists are generally loath to admit it, the accumulation of scientific knowledge is a social enterprise and is, thus, replete with human shortcomings.

Though Kuhn's revelations stirred a great deal of discomfort in the scientific community, nevertheless, his analysis exposed crucial insights about the knowledge accumulation process. Although many scientists insist that the scientific method is founded upon a process of induction--the disinterested amalgamation of isolated facts that gradually expose more general patterns of understanding--Kuhn asserts that "normal science" operates within deductive paradigms: Paradigms are broad, assumption-laden worldviews that supply a theoretical

---

[1]   This is an updated version of an article originally published in *Theory and Science*:
http://theoryandscience.icaap.org/content/vol10.1/McGettigan1.html

foundation into which scientists integrate facts and observations. For example, (while from our 21st century perspective we might be inclined to smirk, nevertheless) devotees of the geocentric paradigm eagerly pointed to the circular motion of heavenly bodies as compelling empirical support for their perspective.

Capable as paradigms may be of illuminating a range of empirical phenomena, they are also plagued by shortcomings. As illustrated by the preceding example, paradigms perform the invaluable service of rendering "the known universe" intelligible and, as a result, paradigms also provide a structure within which knowledge can be organized cohesively and truth-seekers can collaborate constructively. Nevertheless, a paradigm's Achilles heel lies in the truism that the parameters of the known universe are constantly in flux: curious humans incessantly generate novel observations about a constantly changing universe. Again, popular as geocentrism once may have been, an overload of anomalous heavenly phenomena (e.g., comets, retrograde motion, Jupiter's moons, etc.) inevitably doomed the paradigm. When paradigms are overwhelmed by a critical mass of anomalies they enter a phase that Kuhn described as a "crisis." Paradigm crisis is roughly the scientific equivalent of a skipper's signal to abandon ship. Having sprung more epistemological leaks than its adherents can hope to plug, a paradigm in crisis forces its supporters to make fateful decisions: either to jump ship or, having staked out a career upon the foundering vessel, to stay aboard until the bitter end.

Paradigm crisis is a precursor to full scale scientific revolution. According to Kuhn, a scientific revolution comprises a transition through which scientists replace an outmoded paradigm with a new one. Generally speaking, the new paradigm has the advantage of being, so to speak, a more seaworthy vessel, i.e., it resolves many of the anomalies that sank its precursor. Therefore, for a period of time, the new paradigm can confidently go about the process of enlisting recruits and navigating rough scientific seas; that is, until the process inexorably repeats itself and the updated paradigm is gradually beset by its own set of leaks.

Kuhn developed this non-linear view of scientific knowledge accumulation based upon his examination of the history of science. In particular, Kuhn noted that scientific paradigms often incorporate foundational assumptions that are antithetical to the leading assumptions of succeeding paradigms, e.g., one cannot maintain an honest intellectual commitment to creationism and evolutionary theory without suffering from multiple personality disorder. It requires the intervention of an historical revisionist to invent a smooth, linear transition from one scientific paradigm to the next. As such, some critics have asserted that Kuhn's thesis exposed science as a fundamentally relativistic endeavor (Lakatos and Musgrave, 1970). In other words, the fact that successive paradigms tend to be epistemologically contradictory suggests that there is no essential consistency (i.e., no inherent "truth") in scientific progress. That is, if scientific "truth" is linked to the assumptions upon which scientific paradigms are founded and, in turn, if scientific paradigms are disposable, then even in the most rigorous scientific endeavors truth must be only a provisional, transitory standard. In a world of paradigm shifts, truth would appear to be a chimera.

In keeping with this attitude, copious aspersions have been cast on scientific truth--most abundantly from postmodernists. Nevertheless, far from indicating an absence of truth, in this paper I will argue that (r)evolutionary innovations in the structure of scientific knowledge are not an indication of the truth's scarcity. Contrarily, I contend that the process of bringing about paradigm shifts represents the most definitive indication of the scientific commitment to Truth. Distinct as emergent scientific paradigms may appear in comparison to their predecessors, nevertheless, in every case there remain essential "evolutionary" linkages between historic, existing and succeeding paradigms. Indeed, the epistemological relationship between distinct scientific paradigms is "evolutionary" in a similar (metaphorical) sense to the biological speciation process. Just as biological evolution propagates species that appear to have little or no connection to their predecessors (e.g., marine mammals v. their ancient terrestrial forbears), so too do scientific paradigms spawn new epistemologies that appear to lack a clear "genetic" linkage (e.g., geocentrism v. the Big Bang). Though one may have to search to find it, a logical (and, in the case of the philosophy of science, a *social*) connection exists between evolutionarily-distinct constructs. Crucially, for the purposes of understanding the production of truth, it is essential to recognize the manner in which new paradigms, unique as they may be in many respects, generally "speciate" from within the context and tradition of established paradigms.

In spite of the apparent epistemological discontinuity between paradigms, I assert that the production of scientific truth takes place through a process of "redefining reality" (McGettigan 1999, 2002). In other words, truth is not contained within any particular paradigm (as indicated above, by their very nature, all paradigms are riddled with deficiencies), but rather truth guides and enables the process of transitioning from outmoded to "new and improved" paradigms. Also, truth-making never has been and never will be a linear process. Instead, the production of truth is associated with a process whereby individual "agents," upon encountering an over-abundance of environmentally disruptive phenomena (i.e., epistemological anomalies), often develop wildly creative, but nonetheless "adaptive" solutions to resolve the epistemological anomalies they encounter (for example, Einstein's legendary modifications to Newton's mechanical universe). As is the case with evolving organisms, emergent paradigms may appear to be constructs of an entirely new order. Nevertheless, outlandish as they may seem, emergent paradigms maintain demonstrable linkages with their ancestors (e.g., heliocentrism is "a very different animal," but still retains obvious affinities with geocentrism). The difference is that emergent paradigms have been modified through a process of redefining reality to transcend the shortcomings of established paradigms and, thereby, achieve a better "fit" with prevailing environmental conditions (i.e., paradigms evolve through an extensive reimagination process that is intended to reduce anomalies and, thereby, generate a more comprehensive grasp of the ever changing "known universe"). In the balance of this paper, I will demonstrate that such "paradigmatic evolution" is a process that, while spawning epistemological systems of unique and unusual design, is nevertheless propelled throughout by a consistent standard of truth.

Seeing is (Dis)Believing

Mathematicians have their axioms. However, outside the conceptually precise domain of mathematics, it is somewhat more difficult to locate truth. In many scientific endeavors, empirical observation serves as a means to generate and evaluate knowledge claims, e.g., zoologists observe lions and zebras on the African savanna and, by that means, establish (among other things) the truth of their predator-prey relationship. Although Mayo (1933) and Heisenberg (Cassidy, 1991) illustrated long ago that truth in observation has its limits, nevertheless, the relative truthfulness of various knowledge claims is often equated with the degree to which the phenomena at issue are observable. For example, dark matter remained a purely theoretical phenomenon until astronomers identified observable markers of its existence

(Hupp, Roy, and Watzke, 2006). In the social sciences, however, observation has not been universally endorsed as a valid means of identifying truth.

The insistence upon observation as a basis for articulating truth claims--and as a foundation for "good science" (McGettigan, 2002)--is closely associated with a school of thought known as "positivism." Turner (1987) describes positivism as "the use of theory to interpret empirical events and, conversely, the reliance on observation to assess the plausibility of theory" (1987, pp. 156-157). Although positivism has been the subject of extensive criticism, it remains an influential, if not the dominant, paradigm in sociology.

Relying upon observation as a means to evaluate knowledge claims has a strong intuitive appeal. Human judgment is profoundly influenced by sensory observations: we tend to have faith in those things that we can see, smell, hear, taste, or touch, whereas phenomena that defy observation (e.g., the Abominable Snowman) tend to tax credulity. Nevertheless, power elite theorists (Mills, 1956; Domhoff, 2005) have long maintained that observable social phenomena are not reliable measures of truth. Indeed, power elite theorists assert that observable social phenomena are often deliberately distorted by power-brokers with the calculated intention of deceiving observers, e.g., Enron executives projected an illusion of prosperity that, until 2001, most onlookers accepted as "truthful." Therefore, according to this perspective, observable "truths" are often nothing more than cunning fabrications designed by the powerful to deflect attention from their nefarious undertakings. As a result, elite theorists argue that those who maintain faith in the observable world cannot avoid being dupes of the powerful, e.g., Enron made a killing as long as investors remained sold on the company's dissimulations. To get beyond elite-generated distortions, Mills argued, observers need to employ a special form of insight—something he referred to as a "sociological imagination" (Mills, 1959). According to Mills, a sociological imagination is a conceptual framework through which observers can ascertain the impact of invisible social forces--including the handiwork of power elites--on the landscape empirical social reality. Without a sociological imagination, Mills assured, individuals will remain lost in a "welter of confusion."

A Taste for What's on the Menu

Further complicating matters, "radical" power theorists (including postmodernists, among others) have asserted that while elite power-brokers may distort observable reality, an even more insidious form of cultural power tends to subvert the cognition of observers. This is accomplished, Lukes (2005) argues, by creating a dislocation between an individual's real and subjective interests--and induces what Marx identified as a "false consciousness." Essentially, this perspective proposes that a subtle but extremely persuasive form of power cultivates "tastes" (Bourdieu, 1984) in the minds of individual social actors. Such tastes tend to predispose or "encourage" individuals to pursue objectives that seem to be born of individual desire, but that are, in fact, inculcated by prevailing socio-cultural influences.

For example, the cultural context of the early twenty-first century United States tends to inscribe its citizens with a taste for private homes, automobiles, computers, credit cards, cell phones, and fast food (McGettigan, 1999, 2002; Ritzer, 2002; Schlosser, 2001). Generally, we do not view our appetite for such cultural products as the work of social coercion. However, if we were to be situated in a markedly different cultural context, sixteenth century Inuit culture for instance, then our desires would incline toward a passion for warm fur-lined clothing, well-constructed igloos, dog sleds, kayaks, and raw seafood. In the context of pre-industrial Inuit culture, it would be preposterous to lust after Big Macs because the extant cultural system would exert neither the impetus to seek, nor include any of the essential means to fabricate such delicacies. Thus, the third face of power functions as a remarkably effective social glue because of the way that it impels individuals to apply themselves tenaciously to the pursuit of those things that extant cultural systems are designed to provide. Conveniently, these selfsame forces facilitate the reproduction of the cultural context within which individuals are embedded (Willis 1977, Burawoy, 1979): our hunger for automobiles effectively sustains the viability of numerous global industries that are bent on satisfying consumer desires, e.g., petroleum, steel, shipping, etc.

Consequently, as a result of the pervasive influences of radical power, many social theorists have argued that individuals are incapable of observing truth. That is, if every cognitive reference point has been manipulated by cultural power, then any "truths" an observer might identify must be either partly or wholly the product of manipulative social power. Foucault explains:

> ...truth isn't outside power, or lacking in power: contrary to a myth whose history and functions would repay further study, truth isn't the reward of free spirits, the child of protracted solitude, nor the privilege of those who have succeeded in liberating themselves. Truth is a thing of this world: it is produced only by virtue of multiple forms of constraint. And it induces regular effects of power (1980, p. 131).

Thus, Foucault maintains that in every circumstance truth is an instrument of power. From this perspective, truth is a mechanism that is employed to achieve the "positive" goals of a political regime: truth encourages those it influences to "do the right thing", i.e., conform to the will of established authority.

While I agree that, in reality, there is a dynamic, productive relationship between knowledge and power, nevertheless, I believe it is important to emphasize that knowledge and power are distinct phenomena. And given that knowledge and power are distinguishable, even though power effectively distorts most knowledge in reality, it is still conceivable to imagine knowledge that can be constructed independently of the influences of ideological power. If, indeed, there is no knowledge that is independent of power, if truth is wholly the captive and product of power, then truth in every case would have to be the creation of the arbitrary determination of power and it would be impossible for "intellectuals," despite what Foucault suggests, to detach "the power of truth from the forms of hegemony, social, economic and cultural, within which it operates..." (Foucault 1980, p.133). Thus, I maintain that knowledge is not only conceptually distinguishable from power, but, as I will demonstrate, knowledge is also an important vehicle through which power is generated, exercised and, occasionally, undone.

Truth Goes Out of Fashion

It was for reasons similar to those expressed by Foucault that postmodernists asserted there was no longer any virtue in championing universal Truth. Postmodernists pointed out that all knowledge is constructed within bounded socio-cultural systems and, whether characterized as "truth" or not, no form of knowledge could ever be more universal than the social system in which it was created. While this is a markedly different contention than Kuhn's, nevertheless, these points resonate with his characterization of paradigmatic deficiencies: paradigms aspire to compass the "the known universe" but invariably fail due to the contradictions implied in structuring human understanding by way of imposing rigid and, thus, limiting epistemological frames on a fluid and boundless universe. Postmodernists advance the additional criticism that, not only does knowledge tote the baggage of the social context in which it was generated, but it also imposes ideological coercion upon all those who are exposed to it (Lemert, 1991). Proceeding from those assumptions, postmodernists concluded that the modern, scientific "hegemony of truth" was nothing more than a duplicitous justification for Western imperialistic abuse (Seidman, 1991; Lemert, 2004).

As an antidote, postmodernists decided to jettison the notion of universal truth in favor of embracing individual-level truths. This diminution of truth standards remedies what postmodernists perceive as a severe shortcoming in modernist science: throughout the modern era disparate voices had been elided from the pantheon of "valid" knowledge due to the fact that modernist truth standards were (according to postmodernists) excessively coercive and exclusionary. Postmodernists rectified this problem by asserting that all knowledge has an equal claim to truth and validity.

While abandoning universal truth purports to serve a noble purpose, nevertheless, doing so also creates a number of drastic epistemological dilemmas (Sokal, 1996). The first of these is relativism: by abandoning truth standards one foregoes all non-relative means of evaluating knowledge. In other words, in a universe wherein there are no supra-individual truth standards, any knowledge claim by any individual (including luminaries such as Adolf Hitler, Joseph Stalin, Saddam Hussein, and George W. Bush) must be treated as equally valid. Postmodernism establishes no basis upon which to develop and administer broader evaluations of truth (McGettigan, 2000). Ergo, in the absence of grandiose truth standards, one cannot avoid endorsing the machinations of tyrants.

Fleuhr-Lobban (1995) has suggested that, although there are significant difficulties in the specification of universal, supra-cultural standards of truth, it remains the responsibility of social scientists to seek and be guided by such standards. Although Fleuhr-Lobban is well-aware of the dangers that are associated with the imposition of "alien" truth standards, still, she argues that the work of science cannot ignore the misfortunes of the oppressed while also claiming to pursue truth. While Fleuhr-Lobban does not specify a universal standard of truth, she does insist that the implementation of science must not fail to be concerned with justice— or else the search for truth cannot avoid being undermined by the abuses of coercive power. Thus, Fleuhr-Lobban suggests that the development of universal truth standards must be associated with the amelioration of particular injustices both within and across cultural boundaries.

Redefining Truth and Reality

Fortunately, the postmodernist disavowal of truth is the product of a remediable misunderstanding. Once again, postmodernists abjure universal truth (in agreement with Foucault) because of their contention that all knowledge is manipulated by power. However, this viewpoint presumes that power can only influence knowledge negatively: distorting and/or corrupting knowledge and deflecting it from an evocation of undistorted truth. While I agree that the effects of power always modify knowledge, I do not believe that power must always corrupt truth. My basis for this claim derives from a theoretical formulation which asserts that individuals are capable generating truth by "redefining reality" (McGettigan, 1999, 2002).

"Redefining reality" is a process through which individuals can challenge misleading or inadequate paradigms through a combination of astute observation and a creative capacity for ingenious, innovative cognition (i.e., "agency"). As such, via the process of redefining reality, individuals can challenge and negate some of the influences that radical power exercises over their consciousness; redefining reality is a means by which individuals can alter the existing landscape of social reality by creating "spaces" within which they may think and act with a degree of independence from individual, organizational, and cultural social constraints.

The notion of "redefinable reality" posits that there is a universe "out there" that exists independent of human cognition. As such, I argue that "universal Truth" does exist, but such Truth is not (nor will it ever be) contained within extant scientific paradigms. Rather, "The Truth" extends infinitely into the unlocked mysteries of the expanding universe. In other words, reality is what it is: an asteroid is an asteroid is an asteroid, etc... Truth is an intrinsic, inseparable feature of phenomena as they exist independently of human perception. Lies and distortions come into existence via humanity's vast capacity for ignorance: humans view the illimitable universe through awed and flawed psyches. Although admirable in many ways, our grasp of infinite mysteries remains woefully incomplete. Nevertheless, the process of redefining reality permits admittedly limited human minds to make use of empirical anomalies to transcend the limitations of inadequate paradigms in pursuit of a grander vision of Truth.

The process of redefining reality, or overcoming socially-imposed distortions upon knowledge (i.e., including the various shortcomings of existing paradigms) often begins when agents make unanticipated observations, e.g., "Hey! I just looked through my new telescope and it appears as though there are moons orbiting Jupiter!" Individuals may follow up such observations by issuing a challenge to established paradigmatic restrictions, i.e., I guess that means some astronomical objects orbit other heavenly bodies besides earth. In the process of attempting to make sense of such anomalies, individuals tend to deconstruct (Derrida, 1978) the conceptual frameworks that limit their ability to comprehend mysterious phenomena, i.e., based upon what I have observed, I no longer believe earth is the center of the universe. As individuals re-evaluate their beliefs with respect to their inability to comprehend anomalies, the features of their paradigms that do not hold up under scrutiny come under substantial erosive pressure. If individuals are persistent enough, they may reach a point at which the critical mass of their contemplations overloads the shackles of their former beliefs and, thus, they may experience a "moment of truth", i.e., Aha! Planets revolve around the sun, not the earth.

A "moment of truth" is an experience wherein individuals are transported from an inadequate version of reality to a more satisfactory paradigm. These experiences may be considered relatively truthful in that they are generated through a process that involves the intentional negation of ideological controls over an individual's definition of reality. This is not to say that the redefined paradigm at which one arrives after experiencing a moment of truth is, therefore, Truth. Far from that, in keeping with the assertions of radical power theorists (Foucault, 1977; Lukes, 2005), all established belief systems exert their own forms of ideological power on the construction of knowledge. Thus, to experience a moment of truth does not transport one to an ideal realm wherein Truth reigns unchallenged--as opposed to the assertions of Habermas (1970, 1972, 1981). Instead, I merely suggest that the process of redefining reality permits individual "agents" to experience moments of truth within the ideologically-coercive domain of social reality. With the help of such redefined insights, agents become better equipped to negotiate with the pervasive, consciousness-distorting influences of radical power sufficiently to transcend the limitations of established paradigms for the purposes of creating better (but never perfect) paradigmatic proximations of the empirical universe (McGettigan, 2002). Therefore, humans have at their disposal the necessary cognitive mechanism, i.e., moments of truth, through which to take gradual but confident steps toward a broader understanding of the infinite Truths that govern the universe--and, unless I am mistaken, that is and always has been the primary goal of "good science."

Socially-Situated Agency

The fact that agency can be exist in a world of social coercion makes it possible to establish and defend a "socially-situated" definition of truth. The version of "evolutionary truth" that I advocate asserts that no single person will ever arrive at an ultimate representation of Truth. Instead, humans can access narrow, momentary glimpses of truth through the process of transitioning from outmoded to improved definitions of reality. Once again, as scientists (and private citizens) it is essential to embrace coherent truth standards in order to establish a foundation upon which to attack "bad" ideas and replace with them with "better" ideas. In denying the existence of, or requirements for, truth standards, one foregoes any rational basis upon which to rebuke quacks, e.g., tyrants who proclaim that "inferior" people should be exterminated, barstool physicists who profess to know more about relativity than Einstein, or sociologists who contend that all forms of knowledge are equally valid.

According to theoretical formulation upon which the redefinition of reality process is based, in every case it remains up to individual observers to evaluate the veracity of knowledge claims. For example, even the most widely accepted scientific paradigms are, and should be, subjected to intense criticism (Behe, 1996). An environment that invites criticism of even the most popular theories--whether or not we share dissenters' viewpoints--is crucial to the process of progressively and legitimately redefining truth. In other words, dissent is an acid test through which to interrogate good ideas and obliterate bad ones. Once again, no theory produced by humankind either has, or ever will capture "the Entire Truth." Indeed, precisely because of that limitation, the notion of evolutionary truth is an essential means through which to emphasize that even relatively truthful ideas often can and should be supplanted by better ideas.

Indeed, given the foregoing discussion about the limitations of culture-bound knowledge systems, I propose is that eternally provisional, but increasingly proximate paradigms emerge from a negotiation process between:

1. Ingenious, redefining human minds
2. Observable (and, in particular, anomalous) empirical phenomena
3. Established paradigms

Thus, the process of redefining reality implies that "good scientists" can only obtain a competent understanding of the empirical universe by acting as "agents" from within the context of coercive social reality (McGettigan, 1999, 2001). Truth-seekers must directly confront the invisible influences of social power in order to effectively grasp the complexities of the simultaneously contradictory and complimentary relationship between agents and social environments--and, thereby, generate scientific paradigms of increasing veracity.

Evolution v. Extinction

Evolutionary truth is certain to remain unappealing to those who dream of propagating a single, unifying scientific ideology. Nevertheless, evolutionary truth offers a meta-theoretical means through which to build bridges and generate real improvements in every field of scientific inquiry. That is, the notion of refined truth emphasizes that it is possible for advocates of various theoretical perspectives to compromise and collaborate toward the production of ever improving paradigms. For example, from my "evolutionary" perspective, I feel perfectly secure in stating that, despite their numerous theoretical differences, Karl Marx and Max Weber were both brilliant theorists who managed to capture exceedingly valuable insights about the social world they analyzed. Neither theorist was entirely correct nor, I believe, anyone should feel conflicted about drawing upon the strengths of each theory and ruthlessly attacking their weaknesses in an effort to press forward the development of newer, better paradigms. Thus, I maintain that evolutionary truth makes it possible to draw constructively upon the strengths of the vast storehouse of existing scientific knowledge in order to evolve, newer and better definitions of empirical reality. No definition of truth can legitimately claim to offer more, nor should be equipped to accomplish less.

Of necessity, truth must remain an evolving target. As the boundaries of the known universe expand, the paradigms that extend scientific frontiers must keep pace. Humbling though it may be, the surest route to scientific progress is to assume that the existing state of knowledge is lamentable. Whether we like it or not, the grandest truths that we cling to today will eventually seem as quaint as the once firmly held conviction that earth was flat. Indeed, the mere suggestion that any scientific discipline may be nearing an "ultimate theory" (Greene, 1999) is exceedingly curious. No scientific discipline can brag of greater accomplishments than those achieved by physicists. Nevertheless, given that physicists currently acknowledge the universe is permeated by vast quantities of inscrutable "dark" substances, I believe it is premature (to say the least) to assert that ultimate theories lie just around the corner. In fact, rather that being on the verge of an ultimate theory, I would assert that such fragmentary conceptualizations of dark matter and energy auger an impending paradigm shift of epic proportions. When such a paradigm shift inevitably takes place, those who have predicted "the end is near" will be wearing egg on their faces, however, everyone else will benefit from science having taken, yet again, one small (but tantalizing) step toward compassing the universe's far-flung mysteries.

Without doubt, the greatest threat to science is the presumption that any particular paradigm might somehow encapsulate the final, ultimate Truth. In every case where humans have claimed ownership of final truths, agency has been forced to cower in the face of bloody-minded ideology (Barnett, 2006; Bergin, 2006). If scientists are ever unwary enough to presume that their intellectual journey has arrived at its final destination, then in that very moment science, the quest for knowledge and intellectual integrity itself will suffer extinction.

The life of science is necessarily dependent upon an enduring commitment to intellectual evolution. That being the case, scientists can only preserve their enterprise by maintaining an steadfast commitment to agency. In other words, scientists must always maintain a stronger commitment to their own doubts than the "certainties" paradigms tout; scientists must stubbornly seek anomalies that, ultimately, are certain to undermine the cherished paradigmatic beliefs upon which their careers have been founded. This is essential not purely for the purposes of tearing down scientific aspirations--as postmodernists were wont to do. Rather, the goal of accumulating anomalies is to force confrontations between established paradigms and the Truths that transcend those paradigms. Science is at its best when it remains singularly committed to the goal of evolving paradigms and, in so doing, focusing scientists' unwavering aspirations on the Truths that extend perpetually beyond their wildest imaginations.

References

Vincent Barnett, 2006. "Understanding Stalinism: The 'Orwellian Discrepancy' and the 'Rational Choice Dictator'," *Europe-Asia Studies*, May 2006.

Behe, Michael J., 1996. *Darwin's Black Box: The Biochemical Challenge to Evolution*. New York: Free Press.

Bergin, Mark, 2006. "Junk Science". *World Magazine*, Vol. 21, No. 8 February 25 2006.

Bourdieu, Piere, 1984. *Distinction: A Social Critique of the Judgment of Taste*. (Translated by Richard Nice.) Cambridge, Mass.: Harvard University Press.

Burawoy, Michael, 1979. *Manufacturing Consent: Changes in the Labor Process Under Monopoly Capitalism*. Chicago: University of Chicago Press.

Cassidy, David. 1991. *Uncertainty: The Life and Science of Werner Heisenberg*. New York: W. H. Freeman.

Derrida, Jacques, 1978. *Writing and Difference*. (Translated by Alan Bass). Chicago: University of Chicago Press.

Domhoff, G. William, 2005. *Who Rules America? Power, Politics, and Social Change*. 5th Edition. Boston: McGraw Hill.

Fleuhr-Lobban, Carolyn, 1995. "Cultural Relativism and Universal Rights." *The Chronicle of Higher Education*. 41: 39 (June 9) B1-B2.

Foucault, Michel, 1980. *Power/Knowledge: Selected Interviews and Other Writings 1972-1977.* Edited by Colin Gordon. New York: Pantheon Books.

Greene, Brian, 1999. *The Elegant Universe: Superstrings, Hidden Dimensions, and the Quest for the Ultimate Theory.* New York : W. W. Norton.

Habermas, Jürgen, 1970. "Toward a Theory of Communicative Competence." *Inquiry* 13: 360-365.

Habermas, Jürgen, 1972. *Knowledge and Human Interests.* London: Heinemann Educational Books.

Habermas, Jürgen, 1981. *Theory of Communicative Action.* 2 vols. London: Heinemann. Vol. 1, Reason and the Rationalization of Society, also published by Polity Press, Cambridge, England, 1984.

Hupp, Erica, Steve Roy, and Megan Watzke, 2006. "NASA Finds Direct Proof of Dark Matter." *NASA News*, August 21, 2006. http://www.nasa.gov/home/hqnews/2006/aug/HQ_06297_CHANDRA_Dark_Matter.ht ml

Kuhn, Thomas S., 1970. *The Structure of Scientific Revolutions.* Chicago: University of Chicago Press.

Imre Lakatos and Alan Musgrave, (eds.), 1970. *Criticism and the Growth of Knowledge*: Volume 4: Proceedings of the International Colloquium in the Philosophy of Science, London, 1965, (Cambridge: Cambridge University Press, 1970), pp. 231.

Lemert, Charles, 1991. "The End of Ideology, Really." *Sociological Theory* 9: 164-172.

Lemert, Charles (ed.), 2004. *Social Theory: The Multicultural and Classic Readings.* 3rd Edition. Boulder: Westview Press.

Lukes, Steven, 2005. *Power: A Radical View.* Second Edition. London: Palgrave Macmillan.

Mayo, Elton, 1933. *The Human Problems of an Industrial Civilization.* New York: MacMillan.

McGettigan, Timothy, 1999. *Utopia on Wheels: Blundering Down the Road to Reality.* Lanham, MD.: University Press of America.

McGettigan, Timothy, 2000. "Flawed by Design: The Virtues and Limitations of Postmodern Theory." *Theory & Science* 1 (1). http://theoryandscience.icaap.org/content/vol001.001/05mcgettigan.html

McGettigan, Timothy, 2001. "Field Research for Boneheads: From Naïveté to Insight on the Green Tortoise." *Sociological Research Online* 6 (2). http://www.socresonline.org.uk/6/2/mcgettigan.html

McGettigan, Timothy, 2002. "Redefining Reality: A Resolution to the Paradox of Emancipation and the Agency-Structure Dichotomy." *Theory & Science*, 3 (2). http://theoryandscience.icaap.org/volume3issue2.php

Mills, C. Wright, 1956. *The Power Elite*. Oxford: Oxford University Press.

Mills, C. Wright, 1959. *The Sociological Imagination*. New York: Oxford University Press.

Ritzer, George, 2000. *The McDonaldization of Society*. New Century Edition. Thousand Oaks, CA: Pine Forge Press.

Schlosser, Eric, 2001. *Fast Food Nation: The Dark Side of the All-American Meal*. Boston: Houghton Mifflin.

Seidman, Steven, 1991. "The End of Sociological Theory: The Postmodern Hope." *Sociological Theory*, 9: 2 (Fall) 131-146.

Sokal, Alan, 1996. "A Physicist Experiments with Cultural Studies" , *Lingua Franca*, May/June 1996.

Turner, Jonathan, 1987. "Analytical Theorizing." Pp. 156-194 in *Social Theory Today* edited by A. Giddens, and J. Turner. 1987. Stanford: Stanford University Press.

Ulam, Adam B., 1989. *Stalin: The Man and His Era*. Boston: Beacon Press, 1989.

Willis, Paul, 1977. *Learning to Labor: How Working Class Kids Get Working Class Jobs*. New York: Columbia University Press.

Afterword

Postmodernism met its Waterloo in the form of the Sokal Hoax (Sokal, 1996). In brief, Alan Sokal demonstrated that, in abandoning truth, postmodernism rendered itself incapable of differentiating between knowledge and nonsense. Though postmodernists objected to Sokal's tactics, they were unable to launch a credible counterattack. Thus, with one mighty blow, Sokal vanquished postmodernism and claimed victory in the Science Wars.

Unequivocal as Sokal's victory may have been, the future still remains somewhat murky. The pursuit of science and truth is a social process, and is, thus, subject to whim and will of prevailing social trends. For example, the Bush Administration was openly hostile to a variety of scientific initiatives and, as a result, progress was hampered during the first decade of the new millennium. Fortunately, the Obama Administration has reversed many of Dubya's anti-intellectual policies, but there is no guarantee that future administrations will be equally enlightened.

In my next book, *Good Science: The Pursuit of Truth and the Evolution of Reality*, I examine the relationship between truth, science and social change. Though many challenges lie ahead, I argue that the best chance of creating the brightest possible future will only come about as a result of redoubling our commitment to doing good science.

References

McGettigan, Timothy, Forthcoming. *Good Science: The Pursuit of Truth and the Evolution of Reality*. Lanham, MD: Lexington Books.

Sokal, Alan, 1996. "Transgressing the Boundaries: Towards a Transformative Hermeneutics of Quantum Gravity". *Social Text #46/47 (spring/summer 1996)*. Duke University Press. pp. 217–252.

www.ingramcontent.com/pod-product-compliance
Lightning Source LLC
Chambersburg PA
CBHW060154290526
45789CB00003B/1031